CONNECTION
THE NEW CURRENCY

Also by Lisa Marie Platske

Speaking of Success

Designing Your Destiny

Turn Possibilities into Realities

7 Keys to Mastering Connection

Are YOU the Missing Piece?
Don't Leave a Hole in the World

CONNECTION
THE NEW CURRENCY

**How Trailblazers Collaborate to
Build Wealth, Community, and Prosperity**

LISA MARIE PLATSKE

Connection: The New Currency
How Trailblazers Collaborate to Build Wealth, Community, and Prosperity

For more information and to order additional copies:
Upside Thinking, Inc.
5225 Canyon Crest Dr., Suite 71 #154
Riverside, CA 92507
www.UpsideThinking.com

ISBN-13: 978-0-9862817-3-0

Second Edition

10 9 8 7 6 5 4 3 2 1

Dedication

To my sister, Pamela Herman, for being a model of what it looks like to connect authentically and give without expecting anything in return.

To Linda Reifschneider and Becky Whatley, for their vision of the first edition and their faith in me to make it a reality.

Contents

Acknowledgments

While there are countless people who encouraged me to move forward with this project, the following people stand out for their faith in me as I brought this second edition to life.

- **Barbara Dempsey,** my Mom and #1 fan, for encouraging me to follow my heart and teaching me anything is possible;

- **Kendra Cagle,** for her commitment to excellence in book layout and design;

- **Sheri Granneman,** for ensuring the project continued to move forward;

- **Dawn Mena,** for stepping in to wrap up the final pieces of the project;

- **Brenda Rush,** for her expert advice and attention to detail;

- **Viki Winterton,** for her passion helping authors get their messages out into the world;

- **All of the women** who chose to share their stories of deep connection.

I would be remiss if I didn't acknowledge my loving and supportive husband, **Jim Platske,** who encourages me to deeply connect to myself and others. This book would not be complete without his constant encouragement.

Finally, I acknowledge **you**—the reader. This book was written with your journey in mind.

Foreword

"She's the same kind of crazy I am!"

It was my immediate thought when I met Lisa Marie Platske, laughing at how wonderful it was to connect with her.

My second thought, *"She gets everything I teach about the importance of connection to influence,"* was quickly replaced by the realization that Lisa Marie Platske's understanding of the world of connection was well beyond my own. The raw authenticity with which she dove into a conversation with me was astounding and brilliant. I felt 'gotten,' valued and supported within minutes.

In short, I became a massive fan of her work. And it only took minutes. *Connection, The New Currency* quickly became a hallmark of "must read" books I recommend. Because connection is an investment that doubles whenever you spend it.

Lisa Marie Platske has helped me gain a masterful understanding of how powerful authenticity and connection can mobilize amazing and unexpected results in your life. As the founder and leader of an international organization of emerging thought leaders and change agents, putting that understanding into action has achieved amazing results, whether with fellow leaders or with the parking attendant that watches over your car.

Whether you're a powerhouse leader, or simply wanting a more fulfilling life path, *Connection, The New Currency* is the shortcut to high success, joy and fulfillment.

TERESA DE GROSBOIS | Founder and Chair of the Evolutionary Business Council and #1 International Bestselling Author of *Mass Influence - The Habits of the Highly Influential*

Introduction

"I am the connections that I weave."

Aᴛʀɪᴄᴀɴ Pʀᴏᴠᴇʀʙ

Over the past 25 years, I've explored the topic of connection with great enthusiasm and grit. It has benefited me in unexpected ways. Connections have yielded valuable opportunities and introduced me to treasured people.

As I walked through countless trials, I chose to deepen the connection I have with myself, spending time in quiet and discernment. This has enabled me to cultivate deeper and more open connections with others and discover that everyone pretty much wants the same thing—to be valued, loved, and appreciated for who they are.

When I began this project, I intended to create a one-of-a-kind, user-friendly tool to help readers become authentic connectors, the rare people who engage with others without expecting anything in return. Amazing colleagues assisted me in that first endeavor seven years ago.

I chose to create this second edition because of the importance and value of connection and its ability to build wealth, community and prosperity. Because connection is a form of currency, if you understand how to invest and use it wisely, you can reap incredible rewards for yourself, your community and the planet. This book is a collection of stories from women of varying backgrounds, ages, races, and upbringings. My hope is that you will find yourself in their words. The trailblazing women who are featured and who shared their stories for this edition come from incredibly diverse environments, educational experiences and skill sets.

They are educators, CEO's, entrepreneurs, attorneys, non-profit leaders, mothers, sisters, daughters, and wives. Their experiences include working for enterprises ranging from Fortune 500 companies to being solo-entrepreneurs. They are all authentic connectors, women who give freely of their talents and abilities to make a difference in the world. We entrust our stories now in the hope that you will be drawn to the specific chapters and challenges needed for personal growth and individual transformation. We also want to inspire and motivate you to engage with others to form new relationships and networks. It is through the shared exchange of energy and strength that genuine connections change lives.

"We are here to make good things happen for other people. Do that…and you will make good things happen for yourself."

SAM PARKER

◄▲►

Part One

1

The Richness
of Connection

Lisa Marie Platske

*"Life is no brief candle to me. It is a sort of splendid
torch, which I have got a hold of for the moment; and I
want to make it burn as brightly as possible before hand-
ing it on to future generations."*

GEORGE BERNARD SHAW

CONNECTION HISTORY

Our U.S. history is full of stories of our ancestors and the
ways they interacted to produce desired and sometimes unexpected outcomes. As a college history minor, I am interested in what
stories and academics can teach us. In my studies and research, I
discovered a richness of connection woven not only in history but
also in science, art and banking.

Prior to the 18th century, the majority of Americans worked the land, and their harvest drove all aspects of the culture. From sunup to sundown, the daily activities of a farmer, usually the man of the household, were often solitary. His work on the land supported and sustained the family. Helpmates were responsible for cooking early breakfasts of hot coffee, bread, and battered eggs to support their husband's everyday activities. Farm laborers assisting farm owners worked even longer days and had little contact with the outside world. Connections with people were based on work proximity, rather than from conversation with new acquaintances. Bonds were formed by circumstance rather than choice.

The dawn of the industrial age, with its mass-mechanized production, affected patterns of living and working. New forms of power, such as steam, replaced animal strength and human muscle. The Industrial Revolution brought new benefits, including getting more work done and allowing unskilled workers to perform easier tasks. Rapid urbanization followed, as people flocked to cities to work, factories produced goods en masse, and manufacturing companies sprung up throughout the Northeast.

Following the Industrial Revolution, from 1900 to 1918, formally known as the Progressive Era, the U.S. experienced a time of great social reform. New ideas fueled opportunities to gather together. Americans saw the growth of the women's suffrage movement, the campaign against child labor, the fight for the eight-hour workday, and the use of journalism to expose corruption. During this period, almost every aspect of life improved: working hours, working conditions, the overall standard of living…and even connecting. However, the ability to connect within a wider sphere of influence still existed primarily for the educated and elite.

"What we do in life, echoes in eternity."
MAXIMUS DECIMUS MERIDIAS

◂▴▸

Throughout the ages, one constant has been the power of our human connection. Our ability to connect worldwide was previously limited. With the birth of the Information Era, we gained the ability to transfer information freely. Technology, specifically mainstream computer access and the World Wide Web, has allowed rapid global communication to change our society as a whole. Today, we can reach people across the globe within a matter of seconds. The overall impact on the workforce continues to be felt: increased opportunities and higher wages, automation and global competition, and the computerization of tasks that once seemed impossible.

Unlike the Industrial Age, when factory workers were paid to produce, not think, one of the massive changes the computer age brought was the expectation for all employees to think or else settle for low-skill, low-wage service jobs. This effect has produced a spike in entrepreneurship and small business ownership. The trend, as organizations become more reliant on information and less on human capital, leaves a widening gap. Is success possible without any human connection? Or has technology allowed us to be more connected than ever before?

"The rung of a ladder was never meant to rest upon, but only to hold a man's foot long enough to enable him to put the other somewhat higher."

THOMAS HENRY-HUXLEY

◂▴▸

THE SCIENCE AND ART OF CONNECTION

From a scientific perspective, what is the value in connecting? And why do we connect with one person and not someone else? One of the clearest findings to emerge from research is that people are happier when they are with others than when they are alone. We need other people to thrive, whether we are introverts or extroverts. Despite this discovery, it is still unclear why some people just "click" with one another. However, the saying, "We are on the same wavelength," may have some neurological truth.

According to Princeton University neuroscientists Greg Stephens and Uri Hasson in the July 27, 2010 Proceedings of the National Academy of Sciences, brain scans of a speaker and listener who were experiencing a deep connection showed neural activity synchronized during storytelling. This experiment was the first to measure blood flow changes in the brains of two people as they talk. The stronger their reported connection, the greater the overlap between the brains of the speaker and listener. (Keim, Brandon. "Good Connection Really Does Lead to Mind Meld." *Wired Science.* July 26, 2010.)

Connection can also be viewed as an art form. According to the Merriam-Webster online dictionary, the word "connect" comes from the Latin conectere, connectere, from com- +nectere meaning to bind. Choice enters the equation as you get to select the who, what, where, and how of connection just as a painter or sculptor chooses their medium and skillset to create a masterpiece.

Personal decisions highlight individual preference and style. One can decide whether to connect authentically, to connect for personal gain, or not to connect at all. From decisions, an outline of one's life emerges. Like a writer developing a tale with plot, setting, and a host of characters, personal decisions drive life stories.

> *"The last of the human freedoms—to choose one's*
> *attitude in any given set of circumstances;*
> *to choose one's own way."*
>
> VIKTOR FRANKL

◂▴▸

THE MEANING OF CONNECTION

From the perspective of a business owner, I have witnessed a shift in the power of connection. The movement of people getting jobs because of who knows them not whom they know or what they know has increased. Decades of doors opening and closing because of relationships in and out of the workplace has grown into more than simply a "know, like, and trust" factor. With the force of social media, the rules of the game in the technology era have once again changed. We have moved beyond the initial intent of Facebook and Twitter as a forum for connection with family and friends to a full-throttle use of social media that has made transparency across the continents possible. It is not only about connecting, but also about having the ability to express what matters most in the moment.

Through all the noise and chatter, a special group of people exists who use the power of connection to leverage whom they know to open doors for others and genuinely share their gifts with the world. The ruling class that emerges happens between those who network solely for personal gain and those who connect authentically, desiring to do so for a higher purpose, thus making a positive impact on the world. This shift enables connection to be used as a tool for shared influence where everyone who plays the game in this manner has the ability to win or advance.

> *"The miracle is this—the more we share,*
> *the more we have."*
>
> LEONARD NIMOY

◄▲►

THE BANK OF AUTHENTIC CONNECTION

Imagine a large building with a castle-like presence sitting in the middle of hundreds of acres of land. From a distance, you can see the red, green, and white lights from a bustling community—casting shadows on the horizon as the sun begins to set. The beauty of the edifice forewarns you this is no ordinary brick and mortar structure.

As you attempt to put some muscle into opening the hand-crafted oak doors, you discover they glide open effortlessly, showcasing a vestibule and lobby area so breathtakingly beautiful that you begin to rub your eyes in disbelief. The art, tapestries, and simple architecture provide an ambiance, welcoming and serene. It excites you. Although sauntering across the gold-flecked marble floors, you feel as if you are waltzing through the streets of Venice.

Approaching the lone desk, you notice a sign and begin to read, "Please fill out deposit slip here."

Deposit, you think. Deposit what?

Almost as if someone was providing an answer, you notice another sign:

> "Authentic connections only. No connecting for personal gain; no connecting for mutual benefit. The only connections accepted are those with the desire to help others purely because you have the knowledge, talents, gifts, and ability to be of service." [Then you realize this grand building is The Bank of Authentic Connection, and it holds only one account—yours. The form of currency the bank accepts is the currency of "authentic connection." The important question that comes to mind is, "How rich will you be?"

> *"The value of a man should be seen in what he gives*
> *and not in what he is able to receive."*
> ALBERT EINSTEIN

◄▲►

NOTES

_____

_____

_____

_____

_____

_____

_____

_____

_____

_____

_____

_____

_____

_____

_____

_____

_____

_____

_____

_____

_____

_____

_____

_____

_____

_____

2

What *is* Connection

Cynthia Wright

"We make a living by what we get.
We make a life by what we give."

WINSTON CHURCHILL

Many people think of money when they read this Churchill quote. In the past, so did I, which makes sense considering my twenty-year career in the advancement office of a private university. Less than two years ago, that career ended suddenly when the positions of the two associate vice presidents were eliminated. At that point, facing the frightening experience of losing a career I loved, I discovered a deeper level of meaning in Churchill's quote.

During my tenure in higher education fundraising, I performed many community relations functions, including serving on the city's Human Relations Commission, and participating in a variety of chamber and non-profit activities. All those years, I was making community connections on behalf of the university, unaware that I was also making connections that would ignite a transformation in my life when I lost my career. The loss of that career was devastating…for about ten minutes. The community and all those connections caught me before I landed!

A few days into my post-higher-education-fundraising career, I encountered an old friend from my first foray into civic engagement. Jennifer Vaughn-Blakely was a city staff member when I served on the Human Relations Commission two decades ago. She had since become an independent contractor, and she asked, "Have you considered working on your own?" Yes, I had. After the trauma of job loss, the risks of self-employment were not as daunting as before.

Jennifer referred me to one of her own valued clients, Becci Diaz, Executive Director of the Community Settlement Association, who signed the first contract of my new company, The Wright Image. Jim Erickson, a mentor and fundraising legend in our region, recommended me for job interviews and then began to recommend The Wright Image to potential clients. Friends and acquaintances in the Greater Riverside Chamber of Commerce did the same, setting up introductions, and making referrals. My telephone rang incessantly, and people stopped me at meetings to ask about The Wright Image.

My university connections yielded benefits, too. Doug Wible, my counterpart who lost his job the same day I did, recommended me to an arts organization. They became my second client. Later, when he accepted a position as executive director of a health education organization, Doug signed a contract with The Wright Image his first day on the job.

When he received a call from a reporter who was interested in featuring him in an article about his job loss, he asked that she interview me, as well as another terminated staff member. Instead of raging against our former employer, we decided to use the opportunity to recognize and express gratitude to our community. We were photographed in my clo-ffice (that's what I call my half-closet/half-office) and the article led to still more connections. The Wright Image could not have paid for better publicity!

Community engagement does indeed come with a measurable benefit. My first client signed with The Wright Image in May 2009. Within eighteen months, we were working regularly with ten clients, and the calls continued coming.

LINKING UP REQUIRES MORE THAN SHOWING UP

Does this mean an entrepreneur can make an appearance at a few volunteer events and become the darling of the business and civic communities? No, because "showing up" and "connecting" are not synonymous. Joining the board of a non-profit organization to "fluff" a resume or meet prospects is not the same as making an authentic connection.

How do you learn to connect? It is as natural and unconscious as a heartbeat, for some. My friend, Brenda Flowers, is the most enthusiastic connector ever. While many people view the act of making connections as a means to some larger end, Brenda sees the act of putting people together as an end in itself. She is as excited by the looming potential of those introductions as she is when that potential is realized.

I did not realize the source of my own "connector" genes at first. When my father succumbed to cancer, my sister and I chauffeured our mother on the necessary errands that accompany death. As we visited the mortuary, the florist, and the church in the Central California town where my parents lived for almost thirty years, we heard the same comments everywhere we went, "Oh, we see Ed every day when he goes to the post office. We will miss him so much." A few days later, my mother went to the bank and was greeted by tearful bank employees who gave her the same message. Dad had no professional reason to connect in his later years, but he spent those years building connections all over town and beyond.

After all those times I rolled my eyes because Dad refused to miss a day of going to the post office or he insisted on conducting business inside the bank instead of using the automated teller machine, I finally understood he was not motivated by a fear of technology or an odd affection for bills and junk mail. He grew and nurtured a vibrant network of contacts, and I do not doubt that those connections kept him alive longer, as well.

"Those also serve who only stand and wait."

JOHN MILTON

◄▲►

Real connections are organic, nourished through words, actions, feelings, and experiences. Effective connectors possess an uncanny intuition that quickly differentiates between sincere connectors and those who are just "showing up." Connection requires engagement, endurance, and a genuine affection for people and causes. Some connections happen quickly, but the most meaningful ones like those that helped me start my company, are usually nurtured and developed over time.

Connecting is most certainly not a brilliant, new innovation. The art of relating came into being about the time the earth's population surpassed a total of one, but the importance of connecting, like many other principles, must be rediscovered by each successive generation. This principle is difficult to grasp because currently, in addition to connecting instantly around the globe, we also use our cell phones as home intercoms.

Connecting is a highly social activity, and not everyone is open to the same methods of interaction. I am clearly on the extrovert end of the personality spectrum. Occasionally using theatrics, costumes and song to connect and promote causes is fun and has worked for me. It has been a good public relations tool for my business too. As individuals, we have unique personality types as well as the opportunity to explore and discover our most effective ways to connect with others.

Presence, not personality, is at the core of connection. The committee member who stands at the front door of a meeting location and directs guests across the hall to the conference room may be a better connector than the committee member who presides over the meeting. The board member who helps set up tables for a gala event may develop stronger connections than the gregarious member who serves as the mistress of ceremonies.

THE GENDER CONNECTION

If effective connectors come in all types of personalities, does gender play a role, as well? Do men and women connect the same way? When I was in my twenties or thirties, denying any presumption of male superiority, I would have indignantly said, "Of course they connect the same." The more appropriate answer would have been, "Frequently, men and women do not connect the same way," leaving an option for exceptions to the rule while acknowledging the reality of the differences most of us experience.

> *"The good news for women is that business now wants collaborative leadership, relationship skills, sharing of information, and win/win negotiation—skills that come easily to most women."*
>
> NANCY CLARK

◄▲►

Nancy Clark, Founder and CEO of WomensMedia, speaks and writes on the topic of men and women in the workplace (http://womensmedia.com/lunchtalk/2006/04/26/). She says, "We all have anecdotal evidence that we can use to form our opinions, but these could be biased, based on our experiences. I prefer to look at the straight science," which says:

- Male and female fetuses are exposed to different hormones as they are developing.

- Women may have different interactions between the two hemispheres of the brain.

- Men have a better ability to visualize a rotating object than women.

- Men and women employ different hormones in reacting to stress.

Now that we have looked at the science let's return to the anecdotal evidence. I belong to an executive women's networking group that is part of a larger, mostly male, networking organization. Most of the women in the group work for manufacturing companies and sell products; one works for an engineering firm. The group leader is a self-employed, industrial psychologist, but she, too, spent much of her career working in human resources for manufacturing corporations. My background differs significantly from theirs, yet this group satisfies our mutual needs for an exchange of information and ideas. Each meeting begins with a round-the-table update.

Because of our conversations, one of the members who lost her job as a high-ranking executive became a subcontracted researcher for The Wright Image. During another discussion, the group leader recommended one of her former executive peers, now retired, to write for The Wright Image on a subcontractor basis. Many members could tell similar stories about the value of our discussions. How do we connect when our backgrounds and experiences are so disparate? We talk about our careers in-depth, but we also talk about our families, vacations, hobbies, and shoes.

Many of our guest speakers (who frequently speak to multiple groups within the organization) feel compelled to comment on the differences between the female and male groups. Even with work-related topics (e.g., "I finally fired the office manager."), the male networkers do not color in the details, and they rarely mention personal issues, aside from the occasional golf score or vacation itinerary.

Twice a year, the networking groups gather for a large meeting. Introductions are brief, with little, if any, personal information shared with the group. Empirical evidence at my house supports the theory that women connect over a broader spectrum of life experiences and in greater detail. My husband often says, while listening to one of my stories at the end of the day, "I want the short version." That same story conveyed to a female friend, generates follow-up questions and commentary!

In *Group Dynamics* (Wadsworth Cengage Learning, Belmont, CA 2009, p. 253), Donelson R. Forsyth writes that the changes of roles in contemporary society have not erased the behaviors contributing to our perception of the gender differences regarding making connections. Men still tend to be agentic (task-oriented) while women are more likely to approach issues from the communal (relationship) side.

Remember the story about my career transition at the beginning of this chapter? When Jennifer Vaughn-Blakely referred me to her client, she modeled behavior based on relationship and collaboration. Instead of demonstrating possessiveness, Jennifer recognized I could meet a need for that client, and the client could meet a need for me.

Does this mean men do not know how to connect or women cannot focus on a task? Obviously not, but it does mean we must seek balance within ourselves and the groups with which we work. I tell my non-profit clients our work is all about "telling your stories to fund your priorities." The same principle applies to building a for-profit business or simply developing a network of community contacts. The best way to tell your stories is to be present. This is not an invitation to hijack people with your tales, but to engage in collaborative partnerships to align missions for increased impact and funding.

Building useful connections does not guarantee fast results. As a fundraiser, I have many stories about the development of relationships, but my favorite one is a reminder about the endurance factor. The most significant and satisfying contribution in which I was involved during my university career emerged from about seven years of fostering a specific friendship, seeking not just a donation, but a way to honor the donors by helping them make a gift that brought them as much joy as it brought the recipients.

From a sheer economic perspective, the best, most cost-effective marketing or communication tool you have is *you*. A few hours of volunteering each week may equate to thousands of advertising dollars, but, again, a word of caution about motivation: find places that are meaningful to you—not just your bottom line—and then dig in to build long-term connections.

CONNECTION CHALLENGE

Recently, one friend said to another, "Technology helps me connect better with people I knew in ninth grade and who now live out of state, but I find myself connecting that same way with people who are close—people with whom I could interact face-to-face…if I chose to do it." That profound statement should cause us to assess the value of personal connections.

Think about your reaction to an email, as opposed to a handwritten card. Or think about your response to a fundraising letter when compared with your response to a personal request for help.

Would you rather see a text message or hear your friend's voice?

Set goals to test the validity of personal connections. Here are two examples.

- Choose a prescribed period (preferably one to three months) and send similar weekly messages to four different individuals each week: two via email and two handwritten cards. See what kind of feedback you receive.

- Try a new type of community engagement. If all your current involvement is with the chamber of commerce, visit a non-profit board meeting or fundraising event or vice versa. As you explore, take note of the people you see repeatedly—it is a good way to identify excellent connectors.

NOTES

_____

_____

_____

_____

_____

_____

_____

_____

_____

_____

_____

_____

_____

3
The Nature
of Connection
Lynn Forese

"We are all works in progress.
By sharing our worlds, we help one
another make our lives matter."

MARIA SHRIVER

I believe in authentic connections. Even when I did not fully understand why connections were so important, I witnessed them throughout my life. To me, an authentic connection means more than just giving my support and energy but also *accepting* it from others. When I learned to reach out and engage with others instead of putting up a shield, my energy level increased, and so did the balance and fulfillment in my life.

Many times, we women mistake connecting with giving. We focus so much on others that we forget to look at our own needs. We then find ourselves stressed, worn out, or frustrated with our circumstances. As the old saying goes, "If we don't ask, we won't receive." When we help others and ourselves, we get back to our true, authentic nature. And the amazing thing is that when we give, we do indeed receive!

> *"Only through our connectedness to others can we really show and enhance the self. And only through working on the self can we begin to enhance our connectedness to others."*
> HARRIET GOLDHOR LERNER

◀▲▶

My relationships and connections with others have helped me through some of the most difficult and challenging times in my life. I am very appreciative of those people who reached out to connect with me for no other reason than to help me feel supported or loved.

In my quest to understand more about myself and to grow as a person and a professional, I turned to books, seminars, research, and classes on personal development and human behavior. I have learned that life with connection provides a deep experience filled with genuine joy, fulfillment, and meaningful moments. I learned it is our human nature which leads us to connect. But, I did not always understand how essential connections are or how much they add to our lives. I had to unlearn some things to get back to this part of my human nature.

*"We do not accomplish anything in this world alone...
and whatever happens is the result of the whole tapestry
of one's life and all the weavings of individual threads
from one to another that creates something."*

Sandra Day O'Connor

◂▴▸

NATURE VERSUS CULTURE

I was raised in Las Vegas during the '60s and '70s in a large family with all my grandparents, aunts, uncles, and several cousins nearby. I lived in the same neighborhood from the time I was three years old until I graduated from the University of Nevada, Las Vegas, just a few miles from my house. I consider myself blessed to have a strong connection with my family, but this "built-in network," as complete as it was, gave me no reason to reach outside my world.

While we were taught not to ask for favors, on the rare occasions we did, we felt indebted. My mom believed asking for favors meant we were imposing, but in Las Vegas, that was not the case. It was a regular way of sharing. People would ask their friends who worked in casinos for complimentary dinners or shows. You would ask your friend for a show through his "network" of friends, and he would ask you for a show through your friend "network." Those with the most "friends in high places" could take advantage of complimentary amenities because of their networks.

Now that I am older, I realize favor-trading happens everywhere in communities among friends and business associates. It's called networking, and it is natural. And contrary to popular belief, we do not have to run around attending a bunch of networking meetings to make connections.

In addition to not asking for favors, I learned to be a private person. Although I am an outgoing person, I rarely share my thoughts and myself with others outside my family. My built-in set of friends in my family meant I did not have to be vulnerable and share with others outside of my "safe circle."

As I got older and was in the midst of my work life, I felt awkward in situations requiring networking or connecting, especially if I was on the receiving end of help from others. The "art of networking" did not come naturally to me. I always equated networking with "asking for a favor," which I had been taught not to do. Networking also meant you had to share something about yourself, and again, I was much more comfortable keeping my thoughts private. I was uncomfortable at networking events; therefore, I felt they were unnecessary and not valuable. I was just too busy, and I was doing just fine without networking…so I thought.

CONNECTION ADVERSE

When my daughter was four years old, I was living in Arizona and had been a single parent for three years. I had an excellent job, and a terrific boss, but I felt like I needed to be back home in Las Vegas. My daughter, Lindsay, was starting kindergarten, and I wanted her to attend school with her cousins.

One weekend, my childhood friend, Cynthia, came to visit. We were sitting at the kitchen table when I shared my desire for my daughter to have the family support which had been so helpful to me growing up. Cynthia replied, "Well, Lynn, you need to network." I told her I did not have the time. Didn't she realize how busy I was? I was a single parent, already overscheduled, and too exhausted to take any steps for myself. My aversion to connection was based on my misunderstanding of networking.

I appreciated Cynthia's visit, her friendship and even her suggestion that I network to get back home. I did not see how it could happen. I was way too busy, and I felt she did not understand my current situation. Ironically, although I did not buy into Cynthia's theory about networking, I soon found a job in Las Vegas and the issue of relocating resolved.

CONNECTION AWARENESS

Fast forward five years and I found myself working in Scottsdale, Arizona. Although the job provided great career and salary advancement, I was away from home once again. My daughter was now in fifth grade and growing up fast. I knew we needed to move back to Las Vegas where we could have the quality of life we desired near our family. Feeling desperate and lonely about my decision to move to Arizona, I was beating myself up emotionally.

I called Cynthia, who was always a good listener, to share my new dilemma and ask for her advice. I did not want to share my feelings and certainly did not want her to "do" anything to help me because that might be asking for a favor. On the other hand, Cynthia knew me and what type of work I had been doing. She also just happened to be in the Human Resources field, so maybe, just maybe, she knew someone who needed my skills. I wondered if she could make a valuable "connection" for me.

No sooner had I asked for the favor than my phone rang, and Cynthia was on the other end. "Lynn, I found someone who needs you. I was at a women's networking dinner last night and met a fabulous lady who asked if anyone knew someone who had expertise in computers and worked well with people. I leaned across the table, grabbed her hand and said, 'You need to meet my friend Lynn; she knows all about computers.' She wants to meet you!"

That one networking dinner Cynthia attended led me to a terrific job with a great company. This experience helped me finally understand the importance of making connections and developing networks. What I had previously failed to realize was that I had a network outside of my family. I had a network in my circle of close friends. Once I was able to understand this, the next natural progression was to add my business connections to the mix.

"It is not just what you know, and it is not just who you know. It's actually who you know, who knows you, and what you do for a living."

BOB BURG

◂▴▸

REAL CONNECTIONS IN THE BUSINESS WORLD

As a business development professional, my job requires me to make connections and meet new people regularly. I must routinely seek to understand how I can help companies with their business issues and initiatives. Ideally, I deliver excellent service by solving my client's business problems but connecting is at the heart of my work. It allows me to grow my business because people buy services from those with whom they can connect and trust.

HOW CAN WE CONNECT?

Connecting others and connecting *with* others is at the core of our humanity. It's *how* we engage in life, learn more about ourselves, and achieve genuine closeness with others. It is what makes us human. Connecting starts with a sincere interest and curiosity in others. It also starts when we have truly come to value our connections. I am a living example that we can unlearn our past teachings and overcome old habits. I learned we should all make time to connect.

Connecting comes in a wide range of colors and flavors. It involves being curious about other people and what they do or like to do. It's genuinely valuing them as human beings. Connecting is finding out what is going on in a person's life and seeking to know and understand her on a deeper level. Listen carefully, something that is said may lead to another question. If someone tells you, "I am from Los Angeles, but just moved here to Chicago," your response may be: "Welcome to Chicago. I have lived here all my life, and if I can be of any help to you in getting settled, please call on me." This offer is a way to invite sharing and help the other person feel comfortable in continuing the conversation.

At first, this may not be easy. Thinking of simple questions with which to engage others can help. Common interests, hobbies, schools, as well as locations of home and work are all good starting points.

Thank goodness for the lessons I learned from Cynthia and the many other colleagues in my life. They taught me how to network and make connections. I am much better at it now and feel very fortunate to be able to help others.

How exactly do I help? I listen to stories and get to know who people are and what they want to do. I share with others what I know about the landscape of the market and provide information to help them in their journeys. Sometimes, I can forward a resume to a potential employer or even make a hire myself.

While I thought I learned my lesson on networking, the downward economy challenged me to an even deeper level. Many people were out of work and really needed my help with introductions to others or just information about what I might know to help them find their next job. With this focus, I was able to engage at a deeper level with these professionals, and I got the best out of those connections. Not only did I learn how to connect, but during those years, I made it my intention to be more *in the moment* when I met people, so I could figure out how to network for them. I was going to be the "Cynthia" for as many others as possible.

CONNECTION CHALLENGE

Look around you—how can you be a Cynthia for someone? Even if for just one situation, challenge yourself to step out of your comfort zone and speak with someone for the sole purpose of connecting. Do not be concerned that you may not be able to help this person.

Guidelines for your challenge:

- Invest in engaging at least one person for the sole purpose of connecting or networking.

- Do not try to control the outcome.

- Enjoy conversing. Have an overdue lunch with a friend or help your neighbor with a garage sale. Volunteer at a school, church, or shelter. The interaction needs to be for the sole purpose of connecting or "networking to connect."

• During the above engagement, ensure you share something of yourself as well as seek to learn something about the other person(s) with whom you are connecting or networking.

• Be open to what may come of this connection. Be aware you may not have an obvious outcome immediately or even in the next few months. But believe some benefit will come of the interaction, and it surely will.

NOTES

Part Two

4

The Courageous Connector

Lisa Marie Platske

"Each of us has the right and responsibility to assess the roads which lie ahead and those over which we have traveled, and if the future road looms ominous or unpromising and the roads back uninviting, then we need to gather our resolve and, carrying only the necessary baggage, step off that road into another direction."

MAYA ANGELOU

I wish I could say I was born with this magical understanding of the value of connecting, but the truth is I was not always a sharer of knowledge, nor was I a connector. The reality is my life experiences showed me certain rewards for hoarding all the information I had. I excelled in school and in the world of academics, where you are either a "winner" or "loser." Everyone wants to be a "winner," right? Therefore, maintaining an "A" average and not helping others along the way gave me a false sense of being "better than."

Along my journey, I once heard someone say, "Knowledge is Power." I did not translate that phrase into a call to action or use it as the incentive and motivation to study and work harder to gain knowledge and achieve more. Rather, I allowed it to create fear in my life, believing that by withholding my piece to the puzzle, I could control the information others had, making me more important.

As I look back today at how I defined "more than," "better than," and "less than," I am fascinated by how my mind created certain paradigms that affected all my choices, especially how I related to others. I had unknowingly decided at an early age that sharing was not conducive to individual advancement.

"It is our choices that show what we truly are,
far more than our abilities."

J.K. ROWLING

◂▴▸

UNENLIGHTENED

Watching other women around me, I could see many of them had come to the same conclusion. However, in 1997, I discovered the importance of sharing (not necessarily *how* to share) from an unlikely source. A man I worked with at the United States Customs Service in Newark, New Jersey played softball. He participated several times a week and played on three different teams with individuals I knew he did not like. One day I asked why he was anxious to get to the ball field, considering he did not necessarily care for most of the men on the team. He turned to me and asked, "What does liking someone have to do with winning?"

His comment caused an immediate reaction in my brain because it violated everything that had been reinforced in my world; I needed time to process it. Dissecting his remark, I attempted to understand the meaning behind the words. What I discovered was I had always linked the two—liking and winning—which made me initially unable to compute his comment. This was the first of many "aha" moments that led to deeper understanding.

If we choose to connect only with individuals who fit specific criteria or decide not to be a connector at all, can we still succeed in business? Absolutely! However, in an era of continued focus on increased customer service excellence and global partnerships/relationships, our level of success will be stymied by those self-imposed limits.

As I conduct business or coach my clients, I pose the question if a project needs to get done, "Is it more important for all parties to come to the table and accomplish the goal or to like everyone at the table first, and hopefully, accomplish the objective?" The focus is not about like or dislike, liking or disliking, or even being liked or disliked. The *real* issue is, "Are you open to creating a connection with everyone you meet?" Or are you more concerned with making an emotional character judgment before deciding to work together? These are valid questions, and many professionals do not spend enough time asking them.

ENLIGHTENMENT

Working in the field of leadership, I have the opportunity to work with brilliant entrepreneurs, business owners, and executives who understand the need to connect with their management team or their staff, and yet struggle with this concept. One of my clients—an accomplished director—faces this challenge every day and has spent time, money, and energy learning how to connect with others. She has shared with me on numerous occasions that while she understands its place and purpose, she cannot seem to master the art of connection.

Her employees and supervisors are often alienated, and as a continuing part of a negative cycle, she has disconnected herself from them. My client recognizes this causes communication breakdowns, project delays, and departmental turnover. Despite working for the company for two decades, she realizes her position is in jeopardy unless she can build bridges with others and become a connector.

"You can either take action or you can hang back and hope for a miracle. Miracles are great, but they are so unpredictable."

PETER F. DRUCKER

◂▴▸

CHOOSING TO CONNECT

While my softball encounter provided food for thought, I still did not have a full-blown epiphany until I realized the effects my actions had on my relationships at work. My unwillingness to share any information I had with co-workers—whether it was interesting collateral duties, new policies, or opportunities for advancement—created a divide and poisoned my interactions.

At the time, I do not believe I consciously decided to be a "hoarder," but it was a skill and habit I had learned from the many unenlightened colleagues who had gone before me. Choosing not to share information, especially with other women, unless I could use it as a weapon, drew lines in the sand and made it difficult for me to be exceedingly effective and accomplish all I wanted. While I rationalized that I was simply making it obvious whom I respected and wanted to work with, I made character decisions about the behavior I did not like and let it spill over into my ultimate decision not to share information. As a woman in any career knows, showing all your cards can be dangerous…or so I believed. Looking back, I can see my arrogance and ignorance.

"Alone we can do so little; together we can do so much."
Helen Keller

◂▴▸

Over time, I also dissected why I held information so tightly and why my coworker's statement hit a nerve. By listening to my thoughts and the words swirling around in my head, I discovered that sharing of myself, especially participating in a project with people I did not like, no longer made sense. Conventional wisdom teaches that you only connect with people you like, and you only share with people with whom you connect. But how do you find out if you like, trust, or should even connect with someone?

"You accomplish victory step by step,
not by leaps and bounds."

LYN ST. JAMES

◂▴▸

This process took me several years and was a colorful journey. I finally reached the point where I was able to see what was right in front of me. In the beginning, I watched, listened, and learned from many of the men with whom I worked. I focused on speech patterns, phrases, and history with others on the job. While much of my "research" was subjective, my observations led me to conclude that perception and emotional attachment were two major differences in answering the "how" question from above.

THE SECRET

Later, at the Women in Federal Law Enforcement conference in Washington, D.C., I met a man who eventually became my mentor. When we first met, I was impressed by his presence and vowed to stay in contact. His mentorship came through conversations that occurred over many months. During that time, I was seeking advancement in the federal government and turned to him for advice about several positions in which I was interested. He told me I would be perfect for the job in New York, but the vacancy in Washington, D.C. was not a good fit. When I inquired why, he said the people there were not ready for me. It was a nice way of saying, "The political agendas are long, the people do not know you, and you are not quite ready." I vowed to examine what I needed to learn to be a better connector—an authentic connector—with both men and women.

"The secret of joy in work is contained in one word—excellence. To know how to do something well is to enjoy it."

Pearl S. Buck

◄▲►

Upon discovering the "secret," I began to attract the women I could admire and learn from them in ways I did not know were possible. One of these women, who also worked at the U.S. Customs Service with me, opened doors that would never have been possible if I had not been open to the idea of sharing. Through her guidance and support, I gained a better understanding of my job responsibilities and the politics and behind-the-scenes deals that were part of working in the government. When an opportunity arose for advancement, she was the first person to let me know and encouraged me to apply. When a crisis hit, she was the first person to offer assistance and support. Our authentic connection allowed me to grow on the job and advance my career.

I now believe making connections with other women is vital to lasting success both personally and professionally. Women who innately connect bring depth to the level of honesty and courage necessary for creating dialogue, which is very different from communication. Communication focuses on the here and now. It is in the present; it is the conversation we are engaging in at the moment. Connections, on the other hand, are *forward*-focused. Connectors look beyond today to see existing possibilities for influencing future outcomes. They genuinely have a heart for others.

THE CONNECTION

To create an authentic connection, we must be willing to take a risk and be vulnerable. Connectors are fearless individuals who are not afraid to put it all out there—their whole self—and have the world accept or reject who they are. Emotional intelligence is a skill I preach and teach, so I am not saying we permit ourselves to be brash, unkind, or rude. However, I *do* believe we must be confident in being open and understand it may not always be perceived in a way we would ideally like…nor does it guarantee us the outcome we might imagine in an ideal world. Part of taking risks in being authentic requires "connectors" to live a life of complete and utter honesty, which is challenging and hard work.

While I have learned how to lead with deep vulnerability, it doesn't come easy for me. My personal preference would be to only let the world see the things I do well as it feels less judgmental to position myself as having it all together vs. choosing to be fully seen. When I was still working in Federal law enforcement, through the example of one woman who was light years ahead of me in both wisdom and experience, I discovered the courage to take risks, even when it was uncomfortable. I learned how to tell the truth, even if it was not what someone wanted to hear.

This woman later became my mentor and friend. She was a strong woman who valued relationships and honesty; she saw the talents I possessed, and she took a chance. Because of her expert advice and our connection, I was given opportunities and assignments that helped me use my gifts in a way that benefited the organization, as well.

Leaping from being self-protective to being open and walking with daily integrity required a new mindset and new habits.

One of my favorite statements hangs on the wall in my office:

Watch your thoughts, for they become words. Choose your words, for they become actions. Understand your actions, for they become habits. Study your habits, for they will become your character. Develop your character, for it becomes your destiny.

AUTHOR UNKNOWN

◂▴▸

Logically, we may understand the concept that "You get more if you give more," but our behavior shows our understanding of the concept. I have always loved people and making connections, but there was a time I did not always give the best of myself.

Today, I firmly believe the greatest asset one can possess is to learn how to be an authentic connector. It separates the individuals who experience success with those who willingly share their success with others, so everyone wins.

"Then give to the world the best you have and the best will come back to you."

MADELINE BRIDGES

◂▴▸

AUTHENTIC SUCCESS

Without authentic connections with other women, my business would not be where it is today. I own an international leadership company that has grown exponentially over the years. Much of my success can be attributed to the support and guidance of others, including my loving husband. By providing leadership coaching, consulting, and training seminars and workshops, I have transformed thousands of lives and witnessed these leaders fine-tune their individual leadership ability, clarify their personal vision, both inside and outside the scope of organizations, increase their sphere of influence, raise their level of emotional intelligence, change their limiting beliefs about success, and strengthen their long-term growth and profitability. I've created a board of advisors to challenge my growth edges and question my big vision, forcing me to define and re-define where I'm headed.

> *"I have just one chance to live this particular day right, and to string my days together into a life of action, and purpose."*
>
> LANCE ARMSTRONG

◄▲►

In return, through our exchange, I was given the resources and tools to grow. As I've more fully stepped into my role as the CEO of Upside Thinking, Inc., I've discovered how to connect with others in a way I didn't realize was possible. Owning a business has been one of the most challenging and exhilarating experiences of my life, and it's impossible to grow it alone.

Most people want a secret for success. The secret I found comes from being able to connect with others authentically. Authentic connections are born through common bonds, committed relationships, risk-taking, and the desire to see one another succeed.

To get the results I wanted in my business, I had to be willing to change, and this meant continuing to research and deepen my ability to connect with myself, so I could more fully connect with others. Change can be difficult especially when you're out to break an old habit and create a new one. During quiet moments of discernment, I challenged myself to speak up about what I was most afraid of people knowing about who I am. Sharing my biggest fears and failures opened the doors for deeper connection which isn't what I was expecting.

When I shared moments from my personal and professional life, the quality of my relationships grew stronger. First, I began sharing in my blog posts on the Upside Thinker and then on stage at trainings and even in my keynote presentations. Because I realized I couldn't do it all on my own, I intentionally sought out people to connect with who understood what it was like to grow a business.

Choosing individuals to be part of your personal network or mastermind group ensures you won't have to figure it all out alone. The aphorism, "a rising tide lifts all boats" suggests who you hang out with can lift you higher. Every time I lose sight of this truth and make decisions in a vacuum, I can miss something with a costly consequence. A great example of this happened after a decade of hosting my annual Design Your Destiny Live 3-day conference.

Each year, I've been able to turn to my connections and ask them to share their influence, input, and advice. Several years ago, believing the event was running well, I decided to take a new risk and make a big investment in something with a potentially larger payoff. I didn't ask any of my connections for their opinions. At a crossroads, I tried to figure it out by myself, and my business began falling apart. It almost crumbled.

Fortunately, I was able to go back to my connections who cared deeply about my success, and they worked with me to create a plan of action to get back on track. Today, I share these stores at Design Your Destiny Live including some of my biggest failures and traumas. Whenever I make a personal connection, my goal is to be of service and leave the world a bit better by my actions because our deeds affect humanity as a whole.

"Let no one ever come to you without leaving better and happier."

Mother Teresa

◂▴▸

No matter where you are in life, authentic connections can help you achieve that which you never imagined. They enable you to multiply your resources because you made the commitment to connect and were willing to give all you had. The power of connections starts with a willingness to share your gifts and ends in a magnificent creation of something bigger. I do not know of a better way to build wealth, community and prosperity.

"We cannot take credit for our talents. It is how we use them that counts."

Madeleine L'Engle

◂▴▸

CONNECTION CHALLENGE

Take this opportunity to establish your perceived position as a connector. Rate yourself on a scale of one to ten with one (1) being unconnected and ten (10) being super-connected.

Challenge yourself to ask five people who know you well to rate you. Share and discuss your ratings so you can identify areas for future change.

1	5	10
Unconnected	|	**Super Connected**

NOTES

5

The Intentional Connector

Linda Reifschneider

*"I cannot emphasize enough
the importance of a good teacher."*

DR. TEMPLE GRANDIN

EARLY CONNECTIONS

The first woman I ever witnessed connecting was my mother. She has a gift of receiving people as she hosts events. Mom gives her full attention to individuals and focuses on making them feel like they are the most important in the world. Her skill includes genuine interest, eye contact, and active listening. As she leans in, even her body language says, "I am interested in you and what you have to say."

Throughout events, as my mother circulates, she makes sure guests have what they need. She introduces people to each other, and when she finds someone standing alone, Mom asks a question that sparks more conversation and then leads her guests to meet new people in small groups. She makes networking a social art form. I was blessed to observe my mother in action and quickly learned how to make people feel welcome and valued.

Mirroring my mother's example allowed me to work the room effectively, which greatly benefited my professional and personal life. At an impressionable age, I also connected with Jacque, a career woman who happened to be my mother's best friend. She read my writing, listened to my dreams, and invited me to visit for mentoring in the summer between high school and college. Jacque grew into a second mother over the years and remains one of my mentors today.

These two women were my first role models, but for two distinctly different kinds of success: the homemaker and the career woman. Both are successful in their chosen fields, and both are connectors. My mom connected me to women in her life who could lend a hand, provide advice, or model success. Jacque introduced me to other career people. These earliest role models continue to offer their networks to me as I grow through every season of my life.

Both my mother and my mentor showed me early and consistently how making connections is a win-win for everyone involved. Neither one hoarded their networks as something hard won to keep for themselves, but by sharing those connections with me, we each grew. Some women realize the tremendous value of not only networking and giving, but also of reaching out in deep, meaningful, and mutually beneficial ways.

A woman's life is highly interconnected with her family and business. Innate connectors naturally make associations. They intuitively know there will be benefits over time, which will make their lives richer. This currency of connection is so much more valuable than dollars or the growth of our businesses.

CONNECTING IN ALL SEASONS

We all need help at different times in our lives. Divorce, illness, aging parents, job difficulties, and moves to new communities are just a few difficulties we face. The connectors in our lives are the ones who help us get through these troublesome times.

Sheri is one such woman who shared her love, strength, kitchen, and connections with me during a difficult season of my life. Although we belonged to the same organization, we had yet to meet. She was the team captain for a progressive-dinner fundraiser. When I missed an important planning meeting, Sheri called to check on me.

Sensing my profound need, she offered to partner with me to get an assignment done. In the process, she opened her whole life to me, including her faith, and became my mentor. She lived her life in such a way that twenty years later, I came to know Jesus Christ as my savior and am now working to launch my ministry when I retire.

Sheri reached out and pulled me into her network. She taught me how to facilitate and train, which challenged me and helped my career grow. Sheri remains a mentor, sister, and friend whom I can repay by supporting her ministry, as well as increasing her connections with my network. I learned to share more than my network of people. I learned to share my network of skill sets.

*"Tell me and I forget. Teach me and I remember.
Involve me and I learn."*

BENJAMIN FRANKLIN

◂▴▸

We never know where a connection might take us. This book, for instance, is not something I could have ever imagined but resulted because of my relationship with Lisa Marie Platske. A colleague introduced us via email, and we met for coffee. Lisa Marie was new in town and looking for connections. I was in a position to hire trainers for my company. Upon meeting, we instantly bonded. Sometimes you know at a first meeting that you have met a fellow connector when there is mutual honesty, sincere openness, genuine interest, shared ideas, and natural follow-up.

I was able to place Lisa Marie into a few training opportunities, and each interaction brought new depth to our working relationship until a friendship emerged. Years later, Lisa Marie invited me to work on this book project, and now I am a published writer! I have the opportunity to share this connection currency with women I may never meet...planting seeds and not knowing whether or where they might grow.

LIVE THE EXAMPLE

We never know when we will be able to influence someone, and I believe women are obligated to provide an example whenever possible, especially for younger women. One year, I had a young woman work as a student intern for my office. She primarily did office work, but she had so much more potential.

I invited her to chamber networking meetings and started introducing her to people who were working in her field of study. I went above my required internship duties, showed her how to network, and was rewarded by seeing her "get it." She was fully engaged in the process, meeting people, and collecting business cards. I knew someday she would be out in the world building her network. A new connector was born! I will be excited to watch what she does with her life.

Another woman I unknowingly influenced was a student in a management class I taught. This class was particularly difficult because it included several young men who had developed a rather nasty habit of intimidating instructors and bullying classmates. I firmly and directly dealt with the unruly students on several occasions throughout the semester. While it was not pleasant, I could not let these young men run roughshod over me and disrupt the classroom.

At the end of an exhausting, unpleasant semester, a young woman from the class stayed late one night and told me she had never experienced a strong woman in her life. She felt I dealt with the disruptive pair in a manner that demonstrated skills a strong woman could possess while remaining feminine and professional. She believed I had been sent to connect with her. Sometimes a connection exists even when we do not know it, and we can have an incredible impact on others.

"The years teach much which the days never know."
RALPH WALDO EMERSON

⁍▲▸

CONNECT INTENTIONALLY

As a direct result of this project, I have looked at the currency of connection in a whole new way. I took it for granted for the first half of my life because relationships seemed to come so effortlessly to me. My account has been full of this currency! I gave away connections without even thinking about it, watching my account grow without any intentional work on my part.

When I met or worked with someone on a project, pulling my resources was just part of how I worked. For example, a friend was putting together a luncheon to honor women and needed a master of ceremonies. We met for lunch, and the subject came up. I rifled through my mental list of great women MCs and was able to recommend someone who turned out to be just the right person. The event was a grand success, and I was able to help with one tiny suggestion. It was a win for everyone and a home run for her!

Intentional connecting starts with learning basic skills. Make people feel important and teach them how to work the room by taking them along for the ride. Actively showing rather than telling makes the message clearer. It is *living* it, not just speaking it.

When we openly trade in this new currency with no expectation of reciprocity, what we experience is an exponential return. Similar to our faith, when we give, we often gain more than we could have ever imagined. It leaves us with a sense of amazement. We strive to keep giving more and discover in the end that our cup is full to running over.

Sharing a network is just a first step. Sharing skills and growing the skill set of another person builds a legacy that keeps expanding. As each new member is added, greater accomplishments become possible in all aspects of the network because the resources continue to increase. We can enjoy belonging to a massive club, which feels inclusive and seeks to help and promote each other in business, in skills, and in life.

While we may not always know how we impact one another, we need to live the example as we plant seeds everywhere we go. In business, in service, and in mentoring, our impact may not be intentional, but we strive to live each day and treat each contact as though it were. In looking back, I see this web of interaction has been productive. The challenge is to learn, reach, train, share, trade, mentor—to be the *intentional connector.*

CONNECTION CHALLENGE

How can you be intentional today? Select something from this chapter that you feel would be a great place to start...right now! Then, go out and *live* it. Do not worry about being perfect. Just do the best you can.

Where can you connect today and with whom? Who have you seen performing some of the networking skills described in this chapter? That person is more than likely a great person with whom to start. Make a point of introducing yourself and scheduling a time to meet with him or her. Ask for the person's help. Most connectors have the gift of service and respond well to requests.

Once you have made that initial appointment, do your homework. Take an inventory of your contacts and skills. Come to the meeting prepared to share and give. Be ready with questions about contacts you would like to make to help grow your business, network, or skill set. Once you make your needs known, you may be introduced to some people who have extensive networks, thus exponentially growing your own.

Learn about the background and history of the person you are meeting and show a genuine interest in her life and business. You may have a perfect contact to help her. Make sure to bring plenty of business cards to exchange and share. Always ask for at least two business cards from someone whom you recognize is a connector: one to keep and one to pass on.

As you talk and get to know each other, remember the more you give, the more you get. Keep looking for connectors and networkers and repeat this exercise. Soon, you will be known as a connector. You will realize that it happened intentionally instead of accidentally. The next thing you know, a young businesswoman will ask you for a meeting to learn how to grow her network. Not only will you be a connector, but you will also help create one!

NOTES

6

The Successful Connector

Katherine A. Wright

"Example is not the main thing in influencing others; it is the only thing."

ALBERT SCHWEITZER

I was one of ten children, and we moved seven times during my first ten years of life. My father was in the military and was transferred eventually to March Air Force Base near Riverside, California, where he retired, and I settled in for my life. I married a high school classmate, and we've been together for forty-three years.

Growing up, I learned to share and do things for others. During my childhood, I was taught the importance of being honest and trustworthy, as well as the value of hard work and a good education. We had a sense of responsibility to the family and the community.

My parents gave me the opportunity to be part of Girl Scouts and other youth organizations where we were exposed to leadership skills and community involvement—to connect with others in ways that would make a positive impact on individuals and the community. These lessons stayed with me. My parents were good role models and they instilled in me the power of being a good example for others to follow.

> *"A lot of people have gone further than they thought they could because someone else thought they could."*
>
> ANONYMOUS

◂▴▸

For my profession, I chose the K-12 public school system and spent thirty-seven years as a teacher and administrator. For more than two-thirds of those years I held various administrative positions both as an elementary school principal and district office administrator. I worked directly for four different superintendents over seventeen years and spent my last year of service as the superintendent. I was responsible for 20,000 students, 1,500 employees, 21 school sites, and a budget of $149 million. In all my positions, I interacted with students, parents, community members, employees at all levels, and union officials. I also worked with the five-member elected school board, which hired me and represented the district to all kinds of outside business, governmental, and non-profit entities.

Over the years, I met and worked with people who set both good examples and bad examples. Let me say something now about the positive influence those who set bad examples can have. While that sounds like a contradiction, it is not.

In any system, we will always encounter people who conduct themselves in ways that are not a match with our own. We may differ in anything from our overall work ethic to the way we interact with people. In my experience, I encountered people who expected students and staff to work hard and follow the rules even though they did not. I was aware of those in high-level positions making self-serving decisions, wanting respect and special consideration, while treating others disrespectfully. And there were those in influential positions who had regular connection opportunities to make significant improvements, but they dropped the ball repeatedly.

Despite the negative experiences, these people all had a positive influence on me because they were a constant reminder of whom I did not want to be…whom I would never be. Their bad examples motivated me to work hard *not* to be like them.

On the flip side, many people did set a good example for me by exhibiting the highest standards of work quality. They did not expect anything from others that they did not expect of themselves. I experienced many opportunities for professional development involving self-awareness and leadership styles, along with gaining additional technical knowledge and skills.

There are two special people—one male and one female— without whose guidance, mentoring and, yes, sometimes bawling out (a gentle one, but a bawling out nonetheless), I do not believe I would have made it to the top of the organization. Each saw possibilities in me that I did not see in myself. Their belief in me, and willingness to invest in me as a person and employee, along with the relationships we forged, contributed to my success as an accomplished administrator. I am sure without this strong connection—the three of us together—I would neither have been able to earn a doctoral degree while working full-time nor attain any top leadership role in the school district.

Now in retirement, I am still privileged to be involved in connecting activities. I maintain contact with many of my former colleagues in the education arena who continue to turn to me to test out their ideas, ask for advice, and blow off a little steam. Also, I am involved in a myriad of community and civic volunteer activities where the same skill set for making authentic, effective connections applies. Utilizing connecting skills, no matter the arena, leads to the fulfillment of goals and accomplishments in ways that are greater, richer, and beyond what any one person is likely to be able to do alone.

BE YOURSELF

One year, I was invited to attend a retirement party for three teachers I had known for a long time. In our work setting over the years, I was sometimes at odds with these teachers because of the direction the school district wanted to move and my role in affecting that change. The saying "I am from the district office, and I am here to help you," was not always appreciated. The invitation to the party included a comment that I was one of the few people at the district office they liked because I was a "real person." I took that as a compliment. While we may not have always agreed on classroom practices and school matters, they respected me because I was "real."

We've all been told at one time or another when preparing for a job interview, for example, to "just be yourself." At the same time, we must have a sense of self-awareness of how our distinctive ways of speaking, including tone of voice, facial expressions, body language, and manners (or lack thereof), may be seen and received by others. Making successful connections depends in part on how we are perceived.

> *"Whatever is in you can be put to better use*
> *if you learn to connect with people."*
> JOHN C. MAXWELL

◂▴▸

BE GENUINE

As I was working on this chapter, I received a note out of the blue from a woman whom I worked with and supervised for several years. Her note contained words of appreciation for having helped "to navigate my career over the years." I think I first met her when she was a classroom aide working her way through college to earn a teaching credential. She became a teacher, an assistant principal, and eventually a principal.

We easily connected because we shared the same goal of providing a quality education for our students and, more importantly, she was willing to ask for help. I spent time listening to her thoughts, successes, worries, and frustrations, then helped her clarify situations and find options, nudging her toward solutions and action—all the while believing in her as a competent person and educator. Our connection was and still is genuine.

We need to convey with genuine sincerity our interest in others and their success. We do this by spending time to understand their goals and ambitions along with the skills and resources necessary to accomplish them. When we believe in the ability to accomplish those goals, we can give support and encouragement in the process.

LISTEN

Sometime during my career, I picked up an idea for a useful technique when working with people, especially when they are upset about something. I would like to thank the creator, unknown to me, for the success this technique has provided me. For many years, I kept the acronym L.A.S.T. on a Post-it note on my desk for many years. L.A.S.T. stands for:

- Listen to what the person is telling you. It may take a while, especially if the person is emotional and needs time to unwind. Take notes and ask a few questions along the way.

- Acknowledge that the person has a concern, not necessarily that you agree with it or even that it is legitimate. To that person, it is real, so you need to validate that to her.

- Solve the issue, whatever it is, but realize this does not automatically mean you tell her what to do or what you will do to solve the problem, although it might require that step. You may need to explore her options further, including what she can do and what you can do. Not infrequently, by the time the conversation is over, the person has figured things out for herself.

- Thank the person for sharing her issue with you. Usually, it turns out that the other person will thank *you*.

Listening to the other person is probably the most critical principle in successful connecting, but it is frequently overlooked. Often, we are too anxious to tell the other person what we are thinking or what she should do. Instead, try listening to what she is saying or what she is not saying. I passed this handy little tip on to all the principals and many teachers with whom I worked. Try it. I think you will find it's beneficial.

Many teachers and neophyte administrators came to me in my capacity as a senior administrator for advice about their career paths. In talking with them, I took a page from our "backward mapping" curriculum guide, which asks teachers to think backward. What is the desired end result? I asked them where they wanted to be at the end of their careers. What were their ultimate career goals? Once they answered these questions, with a little more nudging, they could figure out the prerequisite experiences and resources needed to accomplish their goals. Of course, "life happens" and along the way goals can be revised as needed.

Asking the right question at the right time is a real art and being able to do so effectively will depend on having first listened carefully. Asking questions helps the other person to clarify her thinking and analyze and define the situation. Although questions can help one identify alternatives, solutions, and potential consequences, questions can also frustrate. After all, the person came to you seeking an answer, a solution or a decision concerning their dilemma. In the long run, though, asking questions helps them gain confidence in their abilities to solve problems and make decisions.

FOLLOW THROUGH

Recently, I found a jacket I wanted to buy at a local department store. It was not in stock in my size, but the store could mail it to my home within two days. The problem was that I'd be out of town starting the next day, and I did not want UPS to deliver a package that would sit on my front doorstep while I was gone for a week. The store clerk offered to make a note on the order that the jacket was not to be delivered until the day after I returned home. I was skeptical, in part because what the clerk was promising to do depended on others following through. But, I agreed to go ahead with her plan. Do you know that the package arrived just as promised? And, the clerk called me to make sure I was satisfied with how the jacket fit. Now, that is doing what you said you will do!

As an administrator, my days were often spent in long meetings or handling duties that took me away from the office for significant chunks of time. I was not always able to return my phone calls the same day or even the next day. If I could not promptly address a concerned parent's call, my assistant would let the parent know I would be in touch as soon as possible. If a lot of time went by between the initial call and my ability to call back, I would have her call the parent, informing her that I had not forgotten and would likely be calling soon. Even parents who were extremely upset and anxious about their situation appreciated hearing back from my office and knowing they were not being ignored. Making such calls likely prevented situations from getting worse while helping my credibility and keeping connections open between parents and the district.

To follow through and do what you say you will do seems obvious as one of the most important things that builds your credibility with others. We have all experienced the lack of follow-through in personal relationships, the work setting, and especially in the wider world, such as in department stores. If you commit to making a phone call, providing information, talking to someone, or offering help in whatever way, you need to follow through. It is a matter of integrity and trust. Do not offer what you cannot or do not intend to deliver. I do not believe you can be a successful connector without taking this principle seriously.

> *Be yourself. Be genuine.*
> *Listen. Ask questions.*
> *Follow through.*

◂▴▸

These connecting strategies helped me throughout my career. Some came natuarlly while others took more practice to master. All of them helped me connect in ways that made me a better leader and helped me accomplish my individual and organizational goals and enjoy success.

CONNECTION CHALLENGE

Now it's your turn. Think of an additional principle you believe will lead to successful connecting. Or maybe you are already living by one. Describe that principle and use it in your next connecting experience.

NOTES

7

The Serendipitous Connector

Lynda-Ross Vega

*"Serendipity is the art of making
an unsought finding."*

PEK VAN ANDEL

In 1994, after twenty-five years in corporate America, I decided to retire from structured business life and engage in the ad-
venture of being an entrepreneur. As my husband Ricardo and I
began the work of creating our first company, I suddenly realized
I did not have a resume. How was that possible? I was an Executive
Vice President of a Fortune 500 company, and yet, I only had a
small bio that appeared in the board minutes and industry publi-
cations. As I reflected on my career, I realized I had succeeded in
corporate life because of the serendipity of connections.

Webster's Dictionary defines serendipity as "the faculty or phenomenon of finding valuable things not sought for"—and that's just what connections have meant in my life. I enjoy people; I am curious about each person's story, and I am either blessed or burdened (depending on your point of view) with a strong desire to help.

My career in the financial industry began as a waitress. True story! I was out of college, newly married, and relocated to a city where my husband had employment. I took a job as a waitress "until something better" came along. For months, people from the bank across the street came in for lunch. We chatted. I remembered their favorite drinks and standard orders.

Then one day, one of the guys said, "You are wasted here; why not apply for a job at the bank?" I was hesitant—after all, what did I know about banking? I had an associate degree in law enforcement, and I doubted that my ability to fingerprint or use self-defense techniques would be valuable assets in banking. However, I accepted his invitation to apply, and the next thing I knew, I had embarked on a career in mortgage lending as an escrow clerk.

A couple of years went by, and one of the vendors I frequently worked with asked whether I was interested in a job opening he was aware of at a much larger mortgage lender. This led to my managing a thirty-two-person mortgage-closing department for a savings and loan. The pattern of my career growth continued.

Every so often, someone I had connected with through work (and perhaps only briefly) would call me out of the blue and offer me a job, taking me to the next level of my career. I transitioned from working on technology projects supporting the mortgage industry to managing large, multi-year projects, to leading a systems and development organization. Each time my career leaped forward, I was quite happy doing what I was doing when a new opportunity presented itself because of a connection.

Was it stroke after stroke of good luck? I do not believe so. Luck plays a part but attracting serendipity into your life is all about being open to connections and nurturing them into authentic ones by first giving something of yourself.

> *"Serendipity is the gift of finding things*
> *we did not know we were looking for."*
>
> GLAUCO ORTOLANO

◄▲►

SOWING THE SEEDS

Now I am not foolish enough to tell you that I like everyone I have ever met or even wanted to maintain a connection with some of them. But, everyone has a story he or she would love to share. By listening to those stories, I discover the common ground on which to build authentic connections. Sometimes, the connection is profound; sometimes, it's fleeting. In either case, the seed for serendipity is sown.

As a budding entrepreneur back in 1994, I knew nothing about marketing. My husband and I bought books on the topic, and we laid out marketing plans. We were determined to succeed, but marketing services is a much different process than marketing widgets (which is what all the marketing books are based on). Stumped, I reached out to a couple of business connections from my corporate past. I asked for advice. "It's all about connections," they said. Surprise! "Call the people you know and tell them you are available and see what happens."

It sounded a bit like "selling" to me, and it made me nervous, but the first call I made proved the power of serendipity once again. "So good to hear from you," was the response I received. "I was thinking about you the other day when one of my clients was sharing a challenge he has. I was going to connect him with you, so that you could give him a bit of advice. But rather than that, how about if you go fix the problem for them?" We had our first client a week later. Not only did our company survive, but it thrives because of authentic connections.

> "Serendipity is putting a quarter in the gumball machine and having three pieces come rattling out instead of one—all red."
>
> PETER H. REYNOLDS

◄▲►

AUTHENTIC CONNECTION CREATES OPPORTUNITIES

Part of the magic of authentic connections is the way they spontaneously create opportunities. The key is to be willing to take advantage of the opportunities as they happen. Sometimes, that causes us to stretch a little bit out of our comfort zone—but that's how we all grow personally and professionally.

Authentic connections, at least for me, rarely happen at networking events where everyone, business card in hand, is trying to sell you on what he or she can do for you. Such activities represent solutions just looking for problems. Those types of events remind me of the speed-dating phenomenon. Both purport to create connections but exchanging business cards or ninety-second elevator speeches rarely generates much of anything other than casual contact. For real connection to happen, you must find a small piece of common ground and then give something of yourself.

When we spun off one of our service offerings into a separate business, my dear friend, Gary Jordan, joined me as a business partner. After twelve years of working with corporate clients, Gary and I decided we wanted to change our focus and work with entrepreneurs, trying our hand at Internet marketing. We signed up for some Internet marketing classes, purchased some home-study kits, and spent some serious money attending a few seminars led by "the experts." The message was always the same: get visible, get a blog, get a website, create an e-zine, use search words, use SEO (I cannot tell you how long it took for me to discover that meant Search Engine Optimization—whatever the heck that is), find joint ventures, etc.

Gary and I spent a lot of time and money getting all the pieces in place. Then we waited and waited and waited. So much for "build it and they will come." Frustration set in, as did self-doubt. Was our product as good as we thought?

Once again, authentic connections made the difference. After monitoring our meager website statistics for a few months, I thought of a woman I had met at an entrepreneurs' conference the previous year. She was vivacious, full of life, and specialized in copywriting. She and I had enjoyed talking about all sorts of things—most of them about dogs and travel and branding—very little about what either of us did for a living. I called her to see whether she would be interested in helping us figure out how to make our web presence successful—maybe point me in the right direction.

She was not just interested, she was enthusiastic! She loved what our business was about, and she turned out to be a wealth of online marketing expertise, as well as an incredibly talented copywriter. Our websites began to sparkle with her help.

Together we developed a great business relationship and a beautiful friendship as well—all due to an authentic connection where real magic began to happen. In the natural course of our association, she has on occasion thought of me when interacting with other entrepreneurs in her circle of friends and put me in touch with them. More connections have evolved for me, and more opportunities have presented themselves. From being a featured speaker to engaging in joint ventures, all have happened because of authentic connections.

ACCIDENTAL WISDOM OPENS DOORS

We owe to a medieval Persian poet the marvelous concept of "serendipity." It is a word born in the delightful Persian tale entitled, "The Three Princes of Serendip."

"[Serendipity] represents a type of accidental sagacity; the faculty of making fortunate discoveries of things you were not looking for."

JAMES J. LYNCH, PH.D.

◄▲►

As a child, I was taught that with age comes wisdom. I am sure that was shorthand for "older people know better" which meant I just needed to do what my parents said without asking so many questions. I remember thinking some magic dust must be part of the birthday surprise that would be sprinkled one day when I was "older," and I would suddenly be wise. Then again, I also remember sitting in the third grade and thinking the year 2000 was so very far away that the whole world would probably be wise by then.

The truth is that wisdom does come when we pay attention to life lessons. Back in 1994, when I was pondering my success without a resume, I attributed much of that success to blind luck—being at the right place at the right time. The reality was that I had sown the seeds for serendipity somewhat unintentionally just by being interested in people, their stories and making authentic connections. The accidental sagacity I have discovered is that authentic connection opens the door for opportunities I would never have known to look for overtly. The primary value of authentic connection in my life is the friendship, shared knowledge, and the fun of knowing interesting people who enrich my life with their stories. The unexpected benefits of authentic connection are the creation of opportunities.

"You do not reach Serendipity by plotting a course for it. You have to set out in good faith for elsewhere and lose your bearings serendipitously."

John Barth

◂▴▸

AUTHENTIC CONNECTION IS THE JOURNEY— NOT THE DESTINATION

Setting out in good faith is the key to authentic connection. We never know for sure where our careers and lives will take us, but the relationships we gather along the way make us better. Regardless of your chosen path, you need authentic connections for the journey. None of us travel our road alone—even as entrepreneurs. Your journey is shaped by the composite of people who touch your life: family, friends, teachers, co-workers, clients, competitors, and strangers on the bus.

Connection experiences make an imprint on you. Without them, you would not be who you are today. As you move forward, authentic connections will add the fun and excitement of sharing and learning; of being valued for who you are. Authentic connections will enrich your day-to-day activities and nurture unexpected opportunities.

The adage *"no man is an island"* is accurate. As human beings, we thrive in community, but wither in isolation. You cannot do it all yourself, no matter how hard you try. Authentic connections provide you with the support and strength of community—the safe harbor to exchange ideas, ask for help, give help, and grow.

No magic formula exists for you to memorize to create authentic connections in your life. All you need is the desire and intention. How easy is that? Open yourself to the possibility. Do you like to be around people? Join a book club, attend a business conference, participate in neighborhood social events, or volunteer for a school or cause you support. Surprising connections will develop with like-minded folks you meet as you learn about each other through conversations and shared experiences.

Do you prefer the comfort of home and social media? Join an online book club, a mastermind group, or an online forum on a topic you enjoy. Seek out a few bloggers with content you like and start commenting, building rapport, and adding value when you can. Amazing connections will develop as you share opinions and questions and ideas. Set out in good faith to expand your knowledge and awareness by listening to the people you meet in the settings you choose; then, authentic connection and new opportunities will happen.

CONNECTION CHALLENGE

This is your opportunity to cultivate the natural serendipity that flows from authentic connections! Start sowing the seeds today. When you are interacting with friends and new acquaintances put the other person first in the conversation. Ask her how she is, what's happening in her life, what she thinks about a particular issue, etc. Give her the opportunity to share with you—and pay attention!

As you listen, offer a piece of information she can use, provide a recommendation, or suggest a resource. Some people will take what you give and move on, but those who will become your authentic connections will be appreciative and become the catalysts for opportunities that come your way.

NOTES

_____
_____
_____
_____
_____
_____
_____
_____
_____
_____
_____
_____
_____
_____
_____
_____
_____
_____
_____
_____
_____
_____
_____
_____
_____
_____
_____
_____
_____
_____
_____

8

The Networking Connector

Becky Whatley

"You give before you get."

NAPOLEON HILL

❧

As the person most responsible for bringing in new business for my company, I have relied almost exclusively on traditional networking for lead generation. Meeting lots of new people in different settings provides a never-ending source of prospects. Networking seems like a fun and straightforward concept: meet people in social business situations so you can do business together. Then you expand the idea: meet people so you can make connections, not just for yourself, but also for others. The way I look at it, anyone I meet, even if that person does not have an opportunity to buy from me, is still likely to be a source of referral or connection later. I meet one person today and tomorrow meet another person. When I realize it would be mutually beneficial for the two to meet, I can make an introduction. This helps me develop a stronger network, set the scene for future business dealings, and initiate those ever-important referrals.

Connecting like this leads the way to the next level: offering expertise. The emphasis moves from "Whom can I sell to?" to "Whom can I help and how can I help them?" Although that may sound altruistic, the truth of the matter is I do it because of the way it makes me feel. What a charge I get from knowing I can make a difference for someone! It is rewarding to be able to make a valuable introduction or spotlight a path not previously seen, and it makes me feel good. Additional rewards can also come from the reciprocal effect. When we reach out to help people, they often want to find a way to help us in return.

The connections I make today are my way of passing along the support I received earlier in my life and career. By focusing on "paying it forward," I invest in a brighter future for someone I may not even know.

EARLY DAYS

My father, Frank, has always been a strong influence in my life. Large and bold, he decided to leave the corporate world to open a print shop in 1982. When I graduated from high school, I began working with him. Together, we learned to run a printing business.

My first experience at networking came while attending industry conferences. Most "veterans" in printing back then were men, so listening to and learning from them seemed natural. It was an extension of the professional relationship I had with my dad.

Soon, however, I started seeking out the women print shop owners. I wanted to talk about my own experience with others like me—women in the business—and not just the married women who provided administrative support to their husbands. I met women who had started businesses themselves or had taken over companies run by their parents. Each year I met more and more of these women, and I found role models with whom I could relate.

At a conference in the '90s, several of my women friends and I started the "PJ's and P&L" party where we gathered in a hotel room in comfy lounging clothes to drink wine, eat potato chips and licorice, and talk in-depth about our financials. Sharing with our peers in an informal setting made discussing complex and personal information (like balance sheets and cash flow) easier. Creating a comfortable space and highlighting the personal connections emphasized the trust we had in each other and encouraged an open exchange of information.

The shared wisdom in a group like this allows us to develop a secure network of allies and resources. Although we are in the same industry, we do not feel threatened or view each other as competitors as we live in different regions. Even those who are competitors in the same geographic area still seem to be supportive and helpful. A natural synergy develops among us. Each woman has a different strength, and collectively, we all can find solutions to the challenges of running our businesses. For example, one who is well versed in technology can answer questions about the best backup strategy for archived customer files. Another contributes tips for personalizing a marketing newsletter.

Keeping in touch between conferences helps us maintain a support network. In many cases, real friendships develop that extend past a professional relationship. Deb from Tennessee and I share evening conversations over wine, even with the three-hour time difference; Cyndy from Nebraska calls me on the weekend when she knows I need cheering up. One year, three of my female print friends joined me in Vegas to celebrate my birthday.

When we converge in Chicago for our annual conference, our conversations buzz with family stories and personal anecdotes as well as business talk. It is a blessing to be able to turn to these women not just for business advice, but also for reassuring comfort, a sympathetic ear, and a soothing word.

"And as we let our own light shine, we unconsciously give other people permission to do the same."

MARIANNE WILLIAMSON

◀▲▶

THE EXPERT WITHIN

During my early days in the industry, I soaked up all kinds of information from the veterans. My interaction with fellow women business owners increased my knowledge and self-assurance. Participating on panels and speaking at workshops confirmed my transition from a greenhorn to a veteran. It surprised me when I realized I had knowledge and wisdom to share. I was an expert!

New members of the printing association began seeking me out for guidance. Conference attendees recommended me for advice on marketing and sales. Succession planning was a hot topic;

parents began asking me to meet with their adult children to give them insight into transition. My shop was not the biggest or the most prosperous, but I had effectively navigated the business waters for more than a decade. I had also successfully transitioned from a young girl working with her dad to a professional print shop owner who read financial reports, understood critical industry ratios, and kept up with the latest trends and technologies.

Realizing I had something to offer, I became eager to pass my knowledge on to others. Sometimes that meant explaining concepts I had learned through seminars. Other times, I would recommend a vendor or product I valued. When I didn't have the needed expertise, I made helpful introductions to others. As new owners opened businesses and next generations succeeded their predecessors, I was able to share experience, offer advice, and give support through mentoring.

In 2003, the National Association of Quick Printers (NAQP) honored me with the Printer of the Year award, the highest honor they give a member. I am proud of this recognition and most gratified because this award is about achievement in making connections. Three of its five criteria are:

- *sharing* knowledge with others in the industry

- *giving back* to the association

- *contributing* to the local business community

I think we naturally look to "experts" for advice and information, rarely stopping to think that perhaps we are the expert to someone else. Become aware of your own expertise, and begin giving your talents and resources to help others.

CONTRIBUTING LOCALLY

Early on, I realized that networking would be a key to local success as well. The Chamber of Commerce, an association dedicated to business success with professionals as members, seemed like the ultimate connection place.

I looked for a mentor as I had in printing. My first impulse was to contact a former printing salesman who had recently taken a position in a different industry. A kind man, he had been approachable as a printing peer, always gracious and helpful. I thought this would be the perfect opportunity to establish the connection I was seeking, but when I asked him to mentor me and help me get the most of my chamber involvement, he thanked me but declined. Instead, he referred me to a woman he respected and admired, someone he believed would benefit me more. He arranged for us to meet, and a few weeks later I found myself at lunch with Debbi Huffman Guthrie, third-generation owner of Roy O. Huffman Roof Company, a business established by her grandfather in 1921.

At lunch we talked as equal business peers, and I found a new level of confidence. Perhaps to Debbi this was just lunch, but to me it was a significant breakthrough. This woman was beautiful and self-possessed; she had style, poise, and wore terrific clothes. Her advice was direct and straightforward: find a committee of interest to me within the chamber and get involved, meet others who share common bonds outside of business.

Debbi became a role model. Her charm and ease at chamber and community gatherings paved the way, helping me gain more confidence at each meeting. She introduced me to new people at every event, pulled me into her circle of influence, and made me feel welcome. Debbi invited me to her Kiwanis Club during the year she was its third female president. A few years later, I joined the same club and in 2009, became the seventh female president in its ninety-year history. I was grateful to have Debbi at my installation.

Although we did not become close friends or establish a conventional mentor relationship, we shared the warmth of interaction. She led by example and inspired me to stretch and reach. She was the human equivalent of training wheels, and when I was balanced and strong enough to ride on my own, she stepped aside. All these years later, I am still honored to know Debbi, and I am delighted when our paths cross on a committee or board.

Besides her impact on my life, both personal and professional, Debbi showed me that establishing authentic connections does not have to be a long-term commitment to be meaningful. It can be as simple, and yet as powerful, as a lunch. Today, as I reach out to others sharing my expertise, I recognize it is the willingness to connect that is more valuable than the amount of time I am giving. That connection can make all the difference to someone. I know it is not necessary to build a close personal relationship for a positive connection to make a tremendous impact.

"The greatest good you can do for another is not just to share your riches but to reveal to him his own."

BENJAMIN DISRAELI

◂▴▸

SHARING WISDOM

Running a business in a small community can create many opportunities for connecting with others. We can pass along hard-earned wisdom and accessible advice. We can share things pertaining to small businesses like the best places for advertising, accounting, and bank rates. We can point out which chamber events are attended by the movers and shakers and which are mostly social. We can recommend restaurants best for business meetings. Sometimes, the actual advice isn't as valuable as our expression of interest in the person who needs encouragement, support, and guidance. Never underestimate the power of a lunch!

Connecting in this way is a significant accomplishment in a professional career. Although success is measured in many ways, I gain fulfillment and a sense of success from knowing that I can offer considerable value to someone else because of my personal experiences and relationships.

As I make that statement, these questions come to mind: "How do you measure achievement? Success? Do you still question your value when it comes to what you have to offer?" As women, we often dismiss our talents by claiming, "It's nothing special" or "Anyone can do it." Yet time and time again, we prove that is not the case.

What we offer is unique and can be a missing piece to someone else's success. What you find comfortable and natural may be a challenge for someone else. Recognizing that skills and talents you possess are unique and essential is a crucial first step to making connections that help others grow and prosper, as well as adding to our wisdom and wealth. Who knows where these connections may take us? Whether a brief exchange or a lifetime relationship, our expertise serves as the platform from which all connections begin.

CONNECTION CHALLENGE

What's your expertise? What is it you do very well? List three talents, gifts, abilities, or skills you believe you possess. Now, write down the names of three people who need what you have to offer. Commit to connect with them in the next six months and share your expertise.

NOTES

_____
_____
_____
_____
_____
_____
_____
_____
_____
_____
_____
_____
_____
_____
_____
_____
_____
_____
_____
_____
_____
_____
_____
_____
_____

9

The Expectant Connector

Dixie McDaniel de Andrade

"Have great hopes and dare to go all out for them. Have great dreams and dare to live them. Have tremendous expectations and believe in them."

NORMAN VINCENT PEALE

Are we not all expecting to find one powerful, authentic connection that will lead us to so much more? As an optimist, I have great expectations for my life and business. Along the way, I have learned when I am authentic with those I meet, ultimately the *right* people come into my life. There is power within authentic communities, and we can expect new possibilities and opportunities to bring deeper meaning to our life and work.

For my story to come full circle, we must begin by going way back to when I was voted "Friendliest" in my high school graduating class. Most people wanted to be known as "Best All Around" or "Most Likely to Succeed," but for me, the word "friendly" meant kind, caring, compassionate, and sharing—all things one strives for in being authentic. I *felt* authentic.

My attitude toward being authentic in business is rooted in the values of faith, family, helping and sharing that I learned at home. I believe when we enjoy what we do in the corporate world and embrace our values, we can achieve financial success. The same can be said of personal interaction. When we stay true to our values and feel comfortable with those we meet, an authentic connection is achieved.

After being in business for many years, I see how the pieces fit together nicely. Writing this, however, I must chuckle a bit at "back then," because I was much more reserved. Now I have two degrees in communication and a passion for speaking, networking, and coaching, not to mention my most important job of being a mom to twins. I am much more headstrong, but still friendly, and that leads to my authenticity shining through a lot more these days.

My mission today is to motivate others to build their businesses and lives and to live in balance. I am a businesswoman who believes in the value of trusted relationships, and I have high expectations our links with one another lead to positive outcomes.

A LASTING INTRODUCTION TO AUTHENTICITY

My first job out of college was as a public relations assistant with a children's hospital foundation, and I had a fantastic boss who turned out to be a long-time friend and mentor. She is an authentic person who embodies my values. She gave me opportunities to work with extraordinary people, gain confidence, and witness the power of connecting authentically. I guess you could say she had high expectations and took a chance on me.

Now, years later, when the two of us collaborate, we can call on the people in our circle to help us produce impressive results. Although our business dealings don't have guaranteed financial gains, because of genuine relationships, we can always count on garnering valuable currency.

A BUSINESS THAT MEANS SOMETHING

My career has involved travel to many countries and continents, as well as international work with accomplished leaders. Traveling and working within cultures different from my own proved to be hard but gratifying work. As a businessperson, I tried to assimilate into the culture and understand how others do business, to relate and be educated by them so I could, in turn, engage in successful business deals. During these years, I learned a great deal about listening and giving of oneself to reap financial rewards.

A colleague from one country said, "I do not know how you do it, but for some reason, these people like you." They did like me…and it was because I listened and learned from them and was always true to myself, and as a result, I enjoyed my years abroad. Working in the non-profit world taught me about the value of being authentic. At times, I stuck out like a sore thumb but was always myself.

I made connections within my business through the trust I built that led to ongoing contracts for the non-profits I supported. Later, those connections led to contracts for my consulting business. These long-term connections remain to this day and are invaluable. I find when we are our authentic selves, we give more and receive so much more.

"What is the meaning of life?
To be happy and useful."
DALAI LAMA

◄▲►

Life in the global development world was so enjoyable, I anticipated always being on the go and laying my head on a pillow in a different country each month. But as life would have it, a change was inevitable. After many years of living a happily married life where both of us traveled, we were doubly blessed with identical twin boys. My business world changed dramatically, and for the best, I may add! I became a mom, and that job became my number one priority. Not wanting to give up on the business world catapulted me into the entrepreneur's world.

Cautiously and hesitantly at times, I began a new type of business life. At first, I made mistakes by trying skills I had not mastered and by veering away from some of my core values. I began a business and was disappointed when the people around me weren't as supportive as I expected. However, I do not call any of my experiences failures since I learned from them. I found my real authentic connections to be the best help to lead me to my true calling.

*"Experience is the name everyone
gives to their mistakes."*

OSCAR WILDE

‹ ▲ ›

CIRCLE OF AUTHENTICITY

You can see how connections have proved immeasurable in my successful consulting business. We value motivation and help companies achieve workplace flexibility, which boosts their bottom line while keeping happy, long-term, great employees. We coach professional women, primarily moms since I am one, to become successful entrepreneurs and live life to the fullest. I also love speaking to groups about the "new" economy, as so many have termed it, and the value of living your dreams.

One of my more recent connections was unable to keep an important speaking engagement, and with her organization's approval, passed the commitment to me. I could not have asked for a more fantastic opportunity to speak and promote my business, so I gave her special thanks in my talk. My presentation stimulated more business thanks to the power of authentic connecting. Plenty of people were qualified to speak to this group, but I was given the opportunity because of a trusted, quality connection built over time. While life is about the big picture, we must not forget the small things of which it is made!

*"We are not cisterns made for hoarding;
we are channels made for sharing."*

BILLY GRAHAM

◄▲►

Building connecting circles with people from various backgrounds and fields is essential, especially if they are in the same business as you. Although we may consider ourselves competitors, we have our unique specialties and collaborating can open doors. As I was building and exploring my coaching/consulting business, I met an experienced coach, and I asked her to lunch. We formed a relationship and collaborated on several events for training and outreach. I have learned from her, and we have both benefitted from one another's circle of contacts. When business women share authentically with one another, competition fades, cooperation emerges, financial success grows, and circles of strategic partners are formed.

CREATING YOUR UNIQUE CIRCLE

What does your unique business circle look like? Does it mirror your personality?

While my business and background may be entirely different from yours, the steps we follow for developing new circles of authentic connection are the same. For example, an initial connection starting with "Hello" may be followed by a compliment or a question. With some more conversation, before we know it, a connection is made, and it is natural to share leads. We may not feel comfortable doing this at first, but with a little faith, when we reach beyond our comfort zones, we expand our networks.

*"Faith is being sure of what we hope for and
certain of what we do not see."*

Hebrews 11:1 (NIV)

◂▴▸

Take time to think about your circumstances and formulate a plan that feels right as you create your community. Most people will tell you networking is the best way to build your circle, and it is indeed a way to meet a large variety of people. Those same folks will also tell you to practice, practice, and practice networking. However, while you may have to practice networking, you do not have to practice being authentic. You are already your authentic self, so get out there and connect with those who will become your most trusted circle. You want to be on someone's list of "Know, Like, and Trust." Trust takes time. Extending yourself to people feels risky, but the benefits are well worth the discomfort.

Remember all those you meet won't be in your authentic circle, but those with whom you develop trust will become part of that circle. Introduce yourself first, not your business, and listen to the person. With a true connection, you are not selling—you are merely simply *being*, and eventually, your connection will do the selling for you.

One piece of advice I can give is always to listen to your inner voice because it is usually spot on. You will know if a connection belongs in your general network or your inner circle. In my opinion, you should always be genuine to everyone you meet even if you do not deepen the connection.

Finally, think about how you would like your circle to look at the end of the day. I mentioned earlier that our network should include those who are in our same business and those who are not, so begin to formulate how your business could take shape or change with the addition of certain people or professions in your network. Seek out ways to meet them.

CONNECTION CHALLENGE

Look at your contact list and put a star beside the people on it you can honestly say are in your Circle of Authenticity. If you have not reached out to them lately, drop them an email or make a call. Keeping up with your most important connections is vital to your success.

The second part of the challenge requires more thought than the first. In the spirit of connecting, collaborating and giving back, seek out a person you have not worked with before and contact them. They may be a CEO, a celebrity, a leader, a neighbor, or an entrepreneur. Send them a letter to share your idea about how the two of you can make a difference for others by donating your unique services.

This exercise works best if the person embodies your values and is possibly in the line of work you want to continue. Be optimistic that you will make an authentic connection because you never know where the power of reaching out can lead until you have the courage to try it. I can guarantee if you make that connection about sharing, your business will prosper. I wish you much luck as you reach out to achieve your great expectations!

NOTES

10

The **Genuine Connector**

Tina Lee

*"We are not human beings on a spiritual journey, but
rather spiritual beings on a human journey."*

DEEPAK CHOPRA

Long ago, I made the correlation that life is about connections,
and by being involved with this book, I now also realize that connections are a currency. Whether we like to admit it or not, the
quality of our connections can significantly determine how the
currency we receive enhances our lives. When I meet new people,
my first thought is not how I can gain financially from this person, but "How can I make her life better?" We all meet people we
instantly connect with, and quite honestly, I am still baffled sometimes by what makes some connections happen so quickly, or why
some connections are naturally much stronger than others.

When we stop to think about it, every aspect of life is about making one kind of connection or another. We make friend connections, business connections, spiritual and love connections. The anonymous quote below shows we have some choice about the people in our lives and the quality of our connections.

"Circumstances (fate or God) determine who walks into your life; it is up to you to decide who you let walk away, who you let stay, and who you refuse to let go."

GET INVOLVED

Throughout my adult life, I have started several groups with the primary purpose of connecting with others for mutual benefit. Many of these groups were women-only groups because I felt the world had plenty of groups for men, but women's groups were not in abundance. I sensed a more significant need for women to connect, sharing all that we have in common and gaining insight and knowledge collectively from our individual experiences in the world. I believe women, in general, make more immediate and stronger connections while men take longer to connect deeply.

My husband has often asked me throughout the years why I get involved in so many groups or activities, and for a long time, I could not answer his question. I only knew that somehow these groups brought fulfillment to my life. The answer is the people—the loving and caring and sharing that comes from involvement with others. Connecting with people brings excitement to my life. I take every opportunity to connect with like-minded individuals, and by doing so, I open my life to many possibilities, both personally and professionally.

One group I started lasted for several years, and eventually, the need for it changed. Several group members began another group that had a different purpose from the first, and after some time, that group evolved into yet another group, leaving behind those who were moving in yet another direction. I have been able to maintain the genuine connections I formed from all the groups.

Each of us would benefit from finding groups with which to get involved. Attend conferences, professional development seminars, and workshops in your area or around the world because the more opportunities you take to meet new people, the more chances you get to make new connections. Attending the same conference or seminar year after year is also a great way to deepen those initial connections.

LUCKY BREAK

When I was growing up, my mother would often say to me, "You do not know how lucky you are." That was most likely quite true. But today, I feel like one of the luckiest people in the world. I am very thankful for all I have, and when I say that, I am not talking about *things*; I am talking about the people I am surrounded by—my friends, my family, my co-workers, as well as my upbeat attitude, my outlook on life, and many more non-material things.

> *"The best things in life are not things."*
> ART BUCHWALD

◀▲▶

Stop and think about your life. What are you doing to ensure you are one of the "lucky" ones? What are the "things" that make you most thankful, and what can you do or change to make your life even better? My connections are a big part of what makes my life great, and the stronger those connections are, the better my life will be.

I have learned that the lucky break does not bring success. Hard work creates a lucky break. Is luck random or inevitable if you take the right approach? Here are ideas to try if you want to create a "lucky break."

- Cast a wide net—It may be random, and you will catch a lot, but by doing this, you are stacking the odds in your favor. Try as many avenues as possible because, in the end, you won't care about what did not work; you will care about the strategy that did work.

- Interact with as many people as you can. Even if you are shy, you can find ways to interact which work for you— like posting comments to a blog or participating on social networking sites. The key is to be genuine because people can tell if you are trying to sell them something.

MAKING STRONGER CONNECTIONS

How do we make stronger, nurturing, and genuine connections and friendships? Like anything else in our lives, what we invest in and give our attention to naturally grows stronger. If we desire deeper relationships, we need to give others what we want. The old sayings of "What goes around comes around" and "You get what you give" remain true today, especially when we look at our relationships. With our connections, therefore, we should apply the Golden Rule of "Do unto others as you would have them do unto you."

If the people around you are not supportive, maybe you should look within yourself and see why you are attracting or connecting with the "wrong" people. Figure out what you want and give that to others so that you will receive it in return. One simple change can make a huge difference!

One way I have found to make more, and stronger connections is to take a chance and share a room with another person when going to a convention, business meeting, or personal outing. We never know how much fun we will have, what we will learn, or what benefits will come from the experience. We all have so much to share.

One experience I had a couple of years ago while attending the Women's Business Conference brought to light the power of connections. I was a first-time attendee and met many great women. The most powerful connection I made came on the last day when I was drawn to a woman with incredible energy. As "luck" would have it, she has a company named Upside Thinking, which intrigued me, and she has written a book about creating the life you want. I bought the book from her, and over the next year, she coached me in my business. She was also the guest speaker in my hometown for a business blast and a women's retreat. The following year, we shared a room at that same Women's Business Conference. She is also the visionary behind this book! Because of our connection, she asked me to contribute to this incredible project, and I am honored and privileged to participate.

RESERVE JUDGMENT

Reserving judgment is another aspect we need to be aware of when making connections. I know this is often easier said than done. We never know what has happened in people's lives to form the beliefs they hold, or how their experiences will dictate the way they react in certain situations. Our first impression of an individual usually stems from physical appearance. Just because someone may not look or dress as society dictates or as we expect, they are still deserving of connection. Some of the most interesting people I have met are the ones I may have shied away from based on their first appearance. Take a chance, make the initial connection, and get to know the person behind the "mask" before deciding whether this is a connection you wish to continue.

Dr. Helen Schucman wrote in the book A Course in Miracles:

You may believe that you are responsible for what you do, but not for what you think. The truth is that you are responsible for what you think because it is only at this level that you can exercise choice. What you do comes from what you think.

Given the verity of Dr. Schucman's statement, since what we do comes from what we think, our attitude must then come from what we think.

"I am convinced that life is 10% what happens to me and 90% how I react to it."

CHARLES SWINDOLL

‹▲›

THE POWER OF ATTITUDE

Our attitude drives our behavior. We oversee our attitude, and we are in control of the decisions we make. When we choose our attitude, we become confident and send out a message others understand, either consciously or unconsciously. When we are confronted with any situation, nothing in the event dictates that we must react one way or another. We choose how it makes us feel and, therefore, how we will respond. Since we do have a choice, most of the time, we will be better off if we choose to react in a positive rather than a negative way.

A study done by two American universities found that people with a positive attitude live longer, healthier lives. The study also found that people who maintain positive attitudes are significantly less likely to show signs of aging, less likely to become frail, and more likely to be stronger and healthier than those who have a negative attitude. Lead researcher, Dr. Glenn Ostir, explained it this way:

> I believe that there is a connection between mind and body—and that our thoughts and attitudes/emotions affect physical functioning, and overall health, whether through direct mechanisms, such as immune function, or indirect mechanisms, such as social support networks.

When you master a more positive attitude, you keep yourself thinking and acting positively, and you will find you make better and more genuine connections.

> *"If you do not like something, change it.*
> *If you cannot change it, change your attitude."*
> MAYA ANGELOU

◄ ▲ ►

CONNECTING WITH FEELING

I have written about different ways to connect, but what about learning to connect with feeling? Not all our initial or ongoing connections are in person. Sometimes they are by telephone, email, or Internet. Many times, new clients who initially contacted me by phone have said they chose me, or my accounting firm, because of the way I made them feel when they called to inquire about our services.

Putting a smile on my face and in my voice lets callers know I am glad to hear from them and would genuinely like to fill their needs. Attitudes come across in our voices. In communication, it is not always what you say, but how you say it, that makes a difference in how the message is heard. Try to convey your positive attitude with your voice inflections, even when you are not feeling so confident.

"I have learned that people will forget what you said, people will forget what you did, but people will never forget how you made them feel."

MAYA ANGELOU

◂▴▸

BECOMING A GENUINE CONNECTOR

To make genuine connections, we need to act. We cannot learn to swim without first getting in the water. Similarly, we cannot make connections without meeting new people or develop genuine, long-term relationships without caring and following up.

I have found the best way to be a genuine connector, and a genuinely caring person is to be friendly, smile, ask questions, and listen to what the person says. If we are connecting for business, we do not just jump right into the business at hand. We first inquire about the other person's life. When meeting a client, I have found making a personal inquiry about her or something special she cares about, helps us form a closer connection. This type of interaction indicates an interest in the person, not just the business. I know a lot of people say we should never become friends with our clients or employees, but I must disagree. I believe in making friends of clients when we have mutual interests.

Giving sincere compliments is another way to be genuine when connecting with family, friends, clients, or those with whom we do business. If something a person says or does impresses you in any way, take the time to let her know. A compliment can be as simple as commenting about her hairstyle or clothing or stating something you have always liked about her. Let her know she is unique and special to you. She will appreciate it, and you will find you naturally get more of the same in return. How simple is that? Life is all about love…the love we give, the love we get, and treating others as we wish to be treated. Remember that one simple thing and you will find you are a better connector and a happier person.

Throughout this chapter, I have conveyed ways of connecting and how to help make those connections better. None of my suggestions will make any difference if you do not look at yourself and figure out what it is you need to do to be a better, more genuine connector. No one can do it for you. You first must commit to yourself. Start with the end in mind and work back from there, and you will instinctively know what to do.

CONNECTION CHALLENGE

For your Connection Challenge, use the list below as you journey toward becoming a genuine connector...today!

- I will join a group of like-minded individuals who meet weekly or monthly.

- I will do business with at least one person this coming year from one of my meetings, conferences or organizations.

- I will practice being non-judgmental by beginning each day with the statement, "Today, I shall judge nothing that occurs, and throughout the day, I'll remind myself not to judge."

- I will daily embrace a positive attitude by choosing to react in a positive rather than a negative way.

- I will treat others as I would like to be treated and give sincere compliments.

NOTES

_____

_____

_____

_____

_____

_____

_____

_____

_____

_____

_____

_____

_____

_____

_____

_____

_____

_____

_____

_____

_____

_____

_____

_____

_____

_____

_____

_____

11

The **Authentic Connector**

Carrie O'Connor

*"Honesty and transparency make you vulnerable.
Be honest and transparent anyway."*

MOTHER TERESA

❦

IT'S ALL ABOUT ME, ISN'T IT?

On the day I found out I passed the bar exam, I also found out I was pregnant with my first and only child. *Yikes!* It was not planned, but it was not prevented either. I chose to "hang out a shingle" with a friend from law school rather than attempt to get a job I knew I would be leaving in nine months. I had never had my own business before, and law school does not teach you about running one. I had examples of entrepreneurs in my personal life, but not lawyers.

We all know being an entrepreneur means we get to wear two hats. First, we get to do what we love. Second, we get to be a business owner. Instinctually, my partner and I knew we had to do something to get the ball rolling. Like most young entrepreneurs, we thought someone in our field should mentor us. We set out to find people who could "help" us.

I first began an internship of sorts with a lawyer practicing criminal law in Orange County, California. His name was Rudolph Loewenstein, a fantastic mentor who led me around the courthouse and jail, let me sit in on his cases, explained the process of new client intake and even let me help on one of his cases. That relationship, although helpful, only made me realize I was not suited for criminal law.

What's the next thing young entrepreneurs do? Apply the shotgun approach, of course! My partner and I attended a myriad of legal functions, trying to meet other small to mid-sized firm owners hoping we would connect with someone to mentor us. Again, we were looking for someone to "help" us. We hit closed door after closed door as we encountered a prevailing attitude of scarcity. People appeared reluctant to lend a hand to a new firm for fear of losing business that could otherwise be theirs. What happened to the "one for all" attitude? Why weren't people lining up to give their time and energy to help us newbies?

Never did we look inward and ask ourselves the question of what we were offering in return. We believed offering our services for free was enough! Never mind that what we were asking them to do would take them three times as long because it required they teach us how to perform a job, while supervising and critiquing us. We were asking for the wrong thing. Instead of asking to shadow a professional, we were asking for free education.

I learned a valuable lesson from this. We always need to examine our motivations. As has become my experience, authentic connections usually are not "one-way streets." We need to evaluate whether we are giving something back in return. If we are not, we probably are not making a long-lasting, valuable, authentic connection.

> *"I do not need a friend who changes when*
> *I change and who nods when I nod.*
> *My shadow does that much better."*
> LUCIUS MESTRIUS PLUTARCHUS

◂▴▸

WHY CAN'T EVERYONE BE JUST LIKE ME?

Successful women are often quite strong, and can sometimes feel threatened by each other. We each have distinct personalities that may or may not mesh. We can adjust them slightly, but we are who we are. Usually, when personalities do not jive, one person feels overrun by the other.

I happen to be one of those strong personalities. I am direct, I do not engage in passive-aggressive actions, and I choose not to beat around the bush. I believe problems should be dealt with before they can fester and turn into something unavoidable. Some call that confrontational. I also think everyone deserves an opinion so long as he or she listens to others' views in return.

These personality traits have been an asset in my business. As an attorney, I am called on to make difficult decisions. I am required to weigh the evidence and present the most viable resolution to my clients. If a settlement does not happen, my clients fully depend on me to represent them. Sometimes, they do not want to hear what I have to say, but it is my job to advise them based on the law and my experience. Judges and opposing counsel have come to appreciate my candor. If I say something, it is because I can back it up. If I provide a settlement figure, it is only after I have listened to opposing points, weighed the evidence, and believe it is fair and equitable. Because of this, I have developed a level of reliance and trust with others. However, over time I have also learned that my behavior may not necessarily elicit the same response from others.

The Golden Rule is an ethical code that essentially stands for the proposition that you should treat others as you would like to be treated and, conversely, that you should not treat others in ways you would not like to be treated. In business, we expect that if we do a good job for someone, she will appreciate it and either do a good job for us in return or pay us appropriately. Similarly, I think we expect that if we act in a particular way, like with honesty and integrity, we will get the same from those with whom we are dealing. This may not always turn out to be the case, which is not always a bad thing, recognizing we are all different and we behave in different ways. For me, an authentic connection occurs over time, allowing me the opportunity to reflect on whether I am willing to accept what I get in return from someone on a long-term basis.

In connecting, my personality traits have sometimes been found to be abrasive and "bitchy." What is interesting is when I encounter another person with the same personality, I *love* it! I feel like we can have a real conversation, and I find it very refreshing to meet someone who will tell me exactly what she thinks.

I call myself *direct* while others may say I am rude. We are all so different, but the end goal of making authentic connections is to have relationships that are not contrived. We do not have to be similar in our traits if we learn to work together and within the boundaries of each other's personalities. We do need to avoid being *fake* or giving in to someone else because of a stronger personality.

Successful, strong women come in all personality types, but when I meet someone who is strong in a passive-aggressive, manipulative way, I want to pull my hair out. Even worse is someone who tells me just what she thinks I want to hear. Typically, I later find out from someone else about how she sincerely feels; then I know she has been gossiping or was not truthful. What occurs in this setting is creating a cycle of resentment.

For instance, I have a friend who says "yes" to everything I invite her to attend. She fears disappointing me. Then, when it comes time for the event, she calls at the eleventh hour to say she cannot make it for some reason. What she does not realize is that I would rather know from the beginning whether she is really intending on coming or not, so I can plan appropriately. This caused a strain in our relationship. When I got annoyed, it reinforced her fear of disappointing me, and round we went.

Learning to recognize the personality types of those we do get along with is important, but even more paramount is understanding the ones of those we do not mesh with so well. We are responsible for adjusting. When my friend wavers with invitations, I have learned to give her an out by saying, "It sounds like you are not quite sure, and I know you are busy. So, for now, I am going to put you down as a no, and if you can make it, great! But, if not, I completely understand."

"No one man can, for any considerable time, wear one face to himself, and another to the multitude, without finally getting bewildered as to which is the true one."

NATHANIEL HAWTHORNE

◄▲►

To make authentic connections, we must first look inward. We must recognize our personality type. First admit to yourself whether you are passive aggressive or a bully, manipulative or forthright, quiet or forceful. Then, *own it!* Let other people know how you are so they know what to expect from you. If you want to make an authentic connection with someone, be transparent. I have warned people countless times of the way I am, and I ask them please not to take offense. When I encounter a situation where I feel I cannot avoid my personality, I ask permission to speak candidly. Finally, I have learned to apologize if I fall into my personality pattern without warning the person with whom I am working.

We can only be responsible for our behaviors and our reactions to the behavior of others. For me, making authentic connections means first admitting who I am, both to myself and to the person with whom I am connecting, and then learning to adjust my response to her personality type.

"If you go out looking for friends, you are going to find they are very scarce. If you go out to be a friend, you will find them everywhere."

ZIG ZIGLAR

◄▲►

SPECIAL THINGS COME IN UNMARKED PACK-AGES

We cannot expect to have a connection with everyone we meet, let alone an authentic one. Authentic connections are special. Yahoo's online dictionary defines authentic as "conforming to fact and therefore worthy of trust, reliance, or belief." In my experience, an authentic connection must be earned by both parties and usually occurs when both parties are transparent with one another. The responsibility is ours to be as authentic as we can be.

My motto is, "Say what you mean *and* do what you say." But, as entrepreneurs, we encounter a lot of "Say what you think others want to hear and do whatever you want." For example, how many times have you heard, "Nice to meet you; I'll give you a call next week." You wait, and the call never comes. I would far rather have people say, "Nice to meet you," and leave it at that if they do not intend to call. Each of us must determine the level of authenticity we will accept from others.

There I was in the business world as a 24-year-old pregnant, new female entrepreneur with a strong personality, who was floundering and striking out left and right. My confidence wavered, and my partner and I were starting to question whether we were cut out to be business owners. We came upon an organization that based its concept of networking on how they could bring value to others rather than how others could benefit them. This concept was not new, but to us, it was undiscovered gold! Through this organization, I made one of the most vital, authentic connections of my life.

I had attended networking meetings before. I knew the drill. You walk around talking to people to see whether they need what you have to offer, and if so, give them your card. It sounds awkward now as I am typing it, but I remember one of the first people I learned from would walk up to someone standing in the food line and say, "Hi, I am (insert name here). Here's my business card." When I first started attending the meetings, I was looking for business. I wanted to find people to hire me to be their lawyer. Isn't that what you are supposed to do as an entrepreneur at a networking meeting?

I found myself looking at people and judging our potential relationship, based on whether I believed they needed my services. In retrospect, that behavior never seemed to garner tons of business, but I never recognized it was the behavior that was the issue until I started learning the powerful underlying principles of benevolent networking—networking based on a desire to help others achieve more in their businesses.

Jo Della Penna of the Business of You was the San Gabriel Valley Chapter President at the time. I admired her for her ability to attract people. She made everyone feel inspired by the time they walked out the door. The message she relayed for the networking group was one coined by Zig Ziglar: "You can have everything in life that you want if you just give enough other people what they want." And she lived it. She seemed genuinely interested in the businesses of others as she actively made referrals and matched people with available services. She spent very little time overtly talking about her own business, although through her conversations, she was adept at letting people know what she did, so that they could keep her in mind as well.

I laugh now because at the time, I did not look to Jo for what she could do for me because I did not believe any possibilities existed. We were not in the same business, nor did she know what I had to do to practice law. She did not need my services. I just assumed she had no idea how to help me. Boy was I wrong! Because of her, my approach to the networking meetings changed, and it became less about getting business and more about learning from the fabulous, experienced women in the group.

When I look back on it, I realize Jo and I connected because I let go of the notion that it was all about someone helping me, and instead, I began to focus on what I could learn. Many times, our lack of authentic connection is due to self-focus. When we first make a connection, if we are too focused on ourselves, we miss what the other person has to offer.

My authentic connection with Jo is transparent. Jo has a way of getting me to be honest with her and with myself. She makes me answer hard questions, and she has me reflect on the reasons behind my decisions. Her openness and honesty allow me to be vulnerable too. When I first met her, I thought she was superwoman. But really, we are all just human. We all have good days and bad, and we all have our struggles.

The life of an entrepreneur is sometimes a lonely endeavor. Often, you are by yourself, trying to navigate territory without a map. Jo's willingness to share that she had some of the same feelings I did about being a young entrepreneur made me feel less alone.

Jo was the initial member of my team of advisors. She joined and became my sounding board even though she was neither a lawyer nor part of my business. She was not even in the legal field. To this day, she offers insightful advice because she has distance from the issues and the business. I only hope I am giving her as much as she gives me in return.

"Be the change you wish to see in the world."

MAHATMA GANDHI

‹▲›

Over time, I have learned several valuable lessons about authentically connecting with other people. The first is that we get a lot more out of our connections with people if we are not so focused on ourselves. The second is that we are each responsible for being our authentic selves, for discovering and admitting who we are, and for learning to adjust our reaction to the personalities and actions of others. And finally, closing yourself off to possibilities because of a perceived incompatibility only serves to limit your number of authentic connections and places limitations on your potential success.

CONNECTION CHALLENGE

Take a long look in the mirror. Are you honest, with both yourself and others, about who you are? The next time you negatively react to someone, examine your reaction, adjust your relationship, and seek an outcome better suited to your personality. The next time you are at a networking meeting, forget you are there to promote your business and focus on learning something about another attendee.

NOTES

12

The **Philanthropic Connector**

Janet Cervantes-Hageman

"Be joyful in hope, patient in affliction,
faithful in prayer. Share with the Lord's people
who are in need. Practice hospitality."

ROMANS 12: 12-13

❧❧❧

We were all put here to serve. Every moment is an opportunity to make a difference when we focus on God, family, and others before ourselves. We each have unique talent, voice, and means. If we listen carefully, the Holy Spirit will put us in the perfect place at the perfect time to serve and to be heard.

I grew up in a small farm town with a great family who taught me to be honest and work hard for everything I would ever have in life. We didn't have much money and I was bullied a lot at school.

For whatever reason, I was tough-minded, set my own goals, and performed to my own benchmarks. It was clear early on that I was on my own to make the life I wanted for myself.

As the first in my family to attend and graduate from college, my determination and hard work paid off. I was told, "Some people run up to an obstacle and go around it, some people climb over it but you Janet, you go through it." I thought that was quite a compliment back then. I was the boss. I called the shots, and if people didn't like it, I didn't care! My attitude was that they can work to earn themselves a seat beside me the same way I did! That attitude carried me up the work merit ladder, but as we all know, no one gets to the top on their own.

Desperately wanting to be successful, I thought I knew what it took to grind it out by working long, hard hours and then working more. I did not make friendships or socialize. I had high expectations, perfectionistic qualities and intolerance for less than optimal performance. I sacrificed time with my family and after marrying at the age of 27 only made time for one child. I would do anything to support and care for my family because I wanted to give them everything!

I worked for a local business owner who was generous to his community. He got me involved in charity and civic work, and I began to invest time in my community on behalf of "our" company.

In October of 2008, I received an email from the Leukemia & Lymphoma Society telling me I'd been nominated as a candidate for Woman of the Year. They wanted to come out and speak to me about it. "Woman of the Year" had a nice ring to it, but I learned this was a fundraising campaign. I would have to compete to win the title by raising the most money in a specified amount of time.

Because I was involved in an automotive dealership acquisition in Omaha, Nebraska, I wasn't sure I had time for the competition.

A few days later, my husband Mike set up a rare family lunch date for the three of us to catch up with one another. During this time, I told my family about the event. Both Mike and our daughter Claire thought it was a marvelous idea, wanted me to do it, and offered to help. I still wasn't sure I had time for it. After lunch, my husband handed me an envelope and asked me to drop it by our bank. It was an important monthly payment for a pool addition on our home.

All the way between the restaurant and the bank my daughter babbled on about how much fun we would have doing this event together. She would get her friends to help. Finally, I told her I would ask ten people to be on my organizing committee, and if all ten said yes without a turndown, I would do it.

As we entered the bank, a beautiful blonde woman walked toward us smiling. There she was, my first ask. I introduced her to my daughter, explained the project and expressed my need for her help with a fundraising committee if I decided to commit. With a broad smile, she told me about how she and the bank manager had talked about nominating me. Puzzled, I asked how she knew about the event as I had not heard much about it. She said that back in April her five-year-old son had been diagnosed with Acute Lymphoblastic Leukemia and was the 2009 Honor Patient for this year's Man and Woman of the Year campaign. I could not believe it!

Here we were in a city of half a million people, and the first person I ask has a direct connection to the cause? What are the odds of that? Then she said the words, "there is no cure for leukemia, only treatment to put the cancer into remission." I felt a call to serve.

When I arrived back at my office, I contacted the Society, asked what the record for the most money raised in the Kansas Chapter was and committed to be a candidate for their event. I formed a committee of fifteen people and in eight weeks raised over $82,000. We funded a blood cancer researcher for a year and set a Chapter record for the most money ever raised by a female candidate in Kansas!

The experience was life changing! I was so touched by how much love and compassion each person associated with the Society had and so impressed by the grit of the patient's families. This woman and her beautiful boy were fighting for his life, and she's at work completing the approval process so that I can have a pool in my backyard? We just don't know what the next person is going through!

That was a pivotal moment for me and for my perspective on the importance of connecting with people on a deeper level. My new philosophy became "every moment is an opportunity to make a difference." The meaning of success changed for me, and it had nothing to do with being named "Woman of the Year."

Following the 2009 campaign, I chaired the Man and Woman of the Year event three times, the Light the Night Walk once and currently sit as the Midwest Chapter Board President. Over the years I've helped raise millions of dollars for blood cancer research and have formed hundreds of relationships with doctors, business owners, and other professionals, as well as with compassionate community people, the kids with cancer and their families. Together we are fighting for the lives of children that can't fight for themselves. We are fighting for parents to get to hold their babies longer until a cure is finally found. Singularly we are limited in what we can accomplish, but together, we are a powerful resource in the fight against blood cancer!

While serving as the Chair of the Light the Night Walk with The Leukemia & Lymphoma Society in September 2012, my husband of 22 years woke up ill with an extreme headache and impaired hearing. I took him to the emergency room that Sunday morning not realizing my life had already changed forever. After 12 hours in the emergency room and hospital, we finally received a diagnosis of a stroke. It was sudden. It was tragic. It was scary. It was only the beginning of what was to come. A week later, after the daily deterioration of his health, Mike passed away. I went through dealing with the news of brain death, discontinuing life support, organ donation and making sure everyone had an opportunity to say goodbye.

As difficult as all that was, I had a funeral to plan, a house full of guests to attend to and stacks of paperwork to complete. In my mourning, I had a grieving, devastated 15-year-old who needed me. She wanted answers and re-assurances that nothing would happen to me. She needed to return to school to catch up, and I had to work. We were now a single income family, after all. There is nothing that will ever compare to the feeling I had watching my life shatter before my eyes. I screamed at God. I was mad!

Claire and I were instantly surrounded by more family than we could manage. Having people around is nice but honestly, when someone dies everyone is dealing with their sadness and grief, so it's a lonely, stressful time. After the initial shock and flurry of activity that accompany a death, people pretty much disappeared. It felt like every move I made was judged. Things heated up as my work demands became more intense and Claire dropped out of everything she'd once loved. My normally clear-thinking mind, hard-charging energy and killer attitude was held hostage by grief and the enormous duties for which I was now singularly responsible. In my devastation and insecurity, I thought I had to act like everything was going to be okay, pretend to be happy, and start my life over. Enter those amazing people I met through my work with the Leukemia & Lymphoma Society.

The parents of the children we had been fighting for, the people I met through the Society and those that were on my team were now the troops supporting me. They brought food, sent cards, took us to events and offered so many kind gestures to us. My Catholic friends prayed rosaries and said Mass for us. It gave both Claire and me hope for happiness as we put back together the shattered pieces of our life. All that giving without any expectation of getting anything in return came back to us, many times over!

"God never ends anything on a negative;
God always ends on a positive."

EDWIN LOUIS COLE

◄▲►

Death and grief could have ruined my life. It could have ended my relationship with God. It could have weakened me to the point of submitting to a life that was meaningless. Somehow though, God put the right people in my path to bring me back to Him. In my new life, I embrace different people and different relationships in a different place. I have dealt with so much and have thankfully discovered loving God and making Him my center-point has brought me through the darkness.

I still have times of sadness, times I miss my old life, but I know who I am and know that God loves me and has a plan for my life. He gave me Mike and gave us Claire. He gave me Mike's family and helped heal some of those relationships. He helped heal most of my family after losing my mom suddenly to cancer shortly after Mike. He helped me find love again with my new husband, Gary, added two sons with wives and three amazing grandchildren. He gave us Gary's thirteen siblings and their parents who have been married sixty-five years! He brought us so much love, Claire and I healed.

Today I try to live my life for God and do things in His name. I try to be open to the Holy Spirit and allow Him to work through me to help others, and in the process, I've found that helping others makes me feel whole and useful. I know it's all about God, but I also know much of my work is because of Mike. I now live for both of us, do God's work for both of us, and love enough for both of us. Because of God's love, Mike lives forever!

This small-town girl has changed. I'm still hard working but I've learned to connect with people by serving them. I've been shown the key to success and surprisingly, it has nothing to do with money or with proving myself. All those years I thought I could do everything by myself. Now I know God is constantly guiding me in amazing ways. His plan was not to ruin my life by Mike's death, but I believe He used it to fill me with more love than I had ever known so I can connect with others through humble service.

"Love must be sincere. Hate what is evil; cling to what is good. Be devoted to one another in love. Honor one another above yourselves. Never be lacking in zeal, but keep your spiritual fervor, serving the Lord."

ROMANS 12: 9-11

◂▴▸

CONNECTION CHALLENGE

Each of us has special talents. Consider your unique gifts and ask God what he wants you to do with them. I challenge you to apply your gifts and your voice to a cause or a charge. There is a person or a charity who needs what you are specifically able to provide. Put everything you have into service and notice how it changes you. Be part of something bigger than yourself! Pray for God to lead you to new opportunities to connect with people through your abundance. What you give will bless you in life-changing ways.

NOTES

Part Three

13

Joining Forces

Janet Steiner

"Coming together is a beginning.
Keeping together is progress.
Working together is success."

HENRY FORD

❦

At the age of forty-five, my dad decided to pursue his dream and start a folding carton manufacturing company. I had already graduated from high school at the time, so I worked as a "volunteer" (more like slave labor) while attending college. Although I eventually took a "career job" in retailing, I regularly helped my dad on my day off during the week.

As the business grew and Dad got busier, he asked if I would come to work for him full-time. I had two issues with this: I liked my retail career and my job paid me.

In time, I was able to convince my dad of the value I could add to the company, and he agreed to match my salary.

Office work did not then, nor does it now, intrigue or inspire me. So, after a few years of being a one-woman office, I asked my dad whether I could go out and try selling.

He said, "Sure. There's the door; there's the world. Go! Just make sure the front desk is covered." Wow, what an education I received. Despite all the hard work and continuous challenges, I grew to love the business. To this day, my passion remains.

> *"A woman is like a tea bag.*
> *You never know how strong she is*
> *until she gets in hot water."*
>
> ELEANOR ROOSEVELT

◂▴▸

We were still a fairly small company when Dad's health failed suddenly, and I was elected to serve as president. I woke up a few days later and realized, *Yikes! So now I'm a CEO, a Controller, a Sales Rep AND responsible for all 40 employees and their families! How did THIS happen?!?*

Oh, and did I mention that folding carton manufacturing is a male-dominated industry? Talk about a lady in hot water! My strength was quickly tested.

GROWING AS A LEADER

As Dad handed over the reins of his dream, he said, "Connect with your industry peers. It's a great way to learn and build trusting relationships. They will be there for you in case of a disaster."

Taking my father's advice, I decided to attend a regional trade association meeting; however, my anticipation and excitement was quickly doused by my peers' cold and unfriendly, "What are you doing here?"

Wow, what a welcome, Jan. Stay cool, be cool.

All energy completely drained out of me. With the instinctive reflexes of a mother, I quickly took stock of the situation and reached for the only successful weapons I had, my feminine charm and off-hand sense of humor. Flashing a smile and batting my eyes, I said, "Uh…my dad had no sons?"

My sales experience had taught me how to deal with rejection, but this…*this* I took as a challenge to my feminine intelligence and the sisterhood in general. I made up my mind to prove a pretty, young blonde *could* be the president of a successful folding carton manufacturing company. Not only would I be running neck and neck alongside "them thar champions," but I was fixin' to kick up some high-heeled dust!

Still hungry to learn and connect with industry peers, I decided to attend the next national trade association meeting. As it turned out, I was the only woman present who was not attending as "a spouse."

One dear lady said to me, "Aren't you glad to be here with your husband?"

Uh…yes, of course! I'm glad to be here with my husband—as opposed to yours or someone else's…

Enjoying my internal joke, I graciously agreed. I did not have the heart (or the nerve) to tell her I was the *principal* there to *learn*—and not "the wife" planning to shop. (Umm, not that there is *anything* wrong with *that*. Trust me. I know how to do some serious shopping! But, as a lady splayed unceremoniously up against a glass ceiling, there's a time and a place for everything!)

> *"Surround yourself only with people*
> *who are going to lift you higher."*
> OPRAH WINFREY

◄▲►

Dedicated to seeing my company grow and prosper, I found the courage to ask the associate staff members whether they could connect me with another independent folding carton manufacturer not situated anywhere near California. They introduced me to the president of a much larger company—although almost everyone was larger at the time— located in Maryland.

Maryland? He's about as far from the West Coast as one can get. This just might work!

We started chatting over adult beverages, secretly sizing up one another. I had so many questions I wanted to ask.

Take it slow, Jan. Make sure he fits in with your strategic plan. Your goal here is to associate with quality leaders who run quality organizations, share similar beliefs, and treat their employees well.

The next day, my husband and I met my new industry peer and one of his key people over dinner. After hearing the way he talked about the business and his employees, I felt this was a man

who shared my passion and values. During the meal, his accep-
tance allowed me to begin asking the questions burning a hole in
my brain.

The ensuing conversation was wonderful and rewarding. Not
only was I learning, but I was also interacting with three men who
treated me as an equal and respected me as a company president. I
remember getting a mini-rush from this first-time experience—*or
maybe it was the cocktails.* Either way, in the mirror of my new
industry peer, I was able to see myself as a CEO—an image I had
not previously been able to envision. For this gift alone, I will be
forever grateful.

During our dinner conversation, I discovered the areas in
which his company appeared to be a strong industry leader and
definitely ahead of us.

*I wonder if he would be willing to allow us to benchmark and
learn from him?*

When I found the courage to ask, he graciously consented and
invited us to his plant for a visit. I was thrilled to have made a connection that would allow us to learn and grow.

> *"Nothing beats the bright lights and
> excitement of the box business."*
>
> NEWTH MORRIS

◄▲►

Back home, we assembled a delegation of four or five people
and flew across the country on a "field trip." Each person had a list

of questions to ask about a particular area of the business. Because our host company was so graciously opening its doors to us, our team was instructed to be open to any of its questions as well.

The trip was amazing. We went home with an education that made us a better company. I remained good friends with my first "industry peer" until his passing in 2018. In fact, we shared many box-making experiences, and I trusted him, even on a personal level. For people to share their trials and tribulations, they first need to trust that the information shared will be only for your edification and not for their harm. Learning from a peer's obstacles and challenges is crucial to avoid the same or similar situation in our own business or personal life. Reciprocal sharing builds a relationship of trust and learning.

THE VALUE OF MAKING CONNECTIONS

A few years later (at the same trade association's meeting), I connected with another president of a non-competing folding carton manufacturer and created an additional learning opportunity for us. Through the years, we have repeated this process time and time again, resulting in continual improvements for our business. Four of us presidents have remained friends, communicating with each other on a regular basis, benchmarking with one another, and serving as a support system in times of trouble. We have developed a trust through which we can ask each other industry questions and openly share our findings.

"Yesterday's home runs do not win today's game."

Babe Ruth

◂▴▸

Over the past years of sharing, I have learned so much from my industry peers: new insights, new possibilities, new materials, new processes and new ways of doing things. Wow! How great is that? We have shared the names of the right people to know in our supply and equipment companies, which is so powerful. We have even shared new products, measuring their success or lack there-of. We were the first company in our group to try a new technology while the others waited to see what the level of success would be. We have also been on the other side, waiting for their approval before we signed on the dotted line.

A trusting connection is not easy to establish. It does not happen overnight; you must take baby steps. Make sure you have agreed to keep everything in confidence before sharing too much. Building trust and building a business takes time, but you will reap the rewards and benefits of well-established connections. Learning this concept will be invaluable.

CONNECTION SPECTRUM

Connections come in all shapes and sizes, and all of them are important. For instance, do not forget your banking partner, who plays a vital role in the growth of your business. Refuse to set-tle for being "just another number!" Know your value and name your price. To explain what I mean, let me share a favorite story with you.

Large companies feel the need to commoditize everything. They develop a bid process including a Request for Information (RFI) to learn more about your company, and then if you are lucky, present you with a Request for Quote (RFQ). We had completed another one of these excruciatingly painful processes with a potential customer when our bank was sold, and we were back to being a number. Using what I had learned from the "big" corporations, I put our banking out to bid!

Our controller and I developed a list of questions to ask, a list of our requirements, and an open section for banks to share what distinguished them from their competition, as well as the "added value" they felt they could bring to us. We assembled this and all the information they needed to know about our company into a professional-looking binder and distributed it to selected banks.

The next thing we knew, the banker parade began! Day after day, "suits" filed in to tour our facility, causing concern among our employees. It was my delight to let them know we were simply looking for a new banking partner, and they were all competing for our business!

The process we initially dreaded turned out to be quite fun. We were in control. Banks were coming to us. Rather than having to struggle (as a small company) to obtain the best program for us, we had them working hard to get our business. The banks most capable of servicing our needs rose quickly to the top of our list, and we were able to negotiate optimum financing for our company.

Changing banks is not always an easy process, so be prepared for a little work on the front end. All your efforts will pay off! Once you find the right financial partner, staying connected to your banker is paramount. Banks do not like surprises. Plan ahead and communicate your financials on a regular basis—including whether you had a good quarter or a bad one. If a quarter was weak, tell your banker why and what you will be doing to improve the next one. Take your banker to breakfast or lunch—your treat. There is always a lot to learn from their perspective. Bankers have great observations, and their comments can be constructive.

We were afforded the privilege to invest in continued growth during a drop in the economy primarily because of the relationship we previously established with our banking partner. You will benefit immensely by staying connected to your banker!

Your attorney is another valuable connection. Attorneys think differently—their many years of schooling taught them how to analyze the pros and cons. Most of them speak legal-ese, so be sure to ask them to explain things in "simple English" terms. They are to your business what a doctor is to your health, so stay connected. The more your attorney knows about you, the better equipped they are to serve your needs. You may not always like what they have to say, but their expertise can save you from yourself at times. Trust me, I know. One of the best ways to stay out of hot water is connecting with your attorney on a regular basis.

If you have not already done so, start taking your CPA to lunch or breakfast at least once every six months. Stay connected. Strategize with them. They will love it. Not only are CPAs aware of the most recent tax incentives, but they have a plethora of knowledge from working with many different companies. On more than one occasion as I reviewed future growth plans with our CPA, he was able to share the accurate insight and information needed to expedite our plan and our growth. You won't regret staying connected to your CPA!

Last but not least, customers are our most critical connections. VOC (voice of customer) is essential, so spend time with your customers on a regular basis. Learn what is in their future and how you can best serve them. This information is critical when developing plans for your company. Also, share with your customers the latest market developments to assist in *their* sales growth. I have made it a practice to remind our employees on a regular basis that their paycheck is compliments of the customer. Never lose touch with your customers; stay connected.

"Family is the most important thing in the world."

Diana Spencer

◂▴▸

Although not directly related to your business, your success rides on the top priority of staying connected with your family. They are your grounding and foundation. Enjoy them and have fun with them. Ultimately, our families are the ones who will be there for us. It is important to share with them the basics of your business life, but they do not need to be burdened with all the details.

"Leadership and learning are
indispensable to each other."

John Fitzgerald Kennedy

◂▴▸

LEARNING BY CONNECTING

Staying at the top of your game requires continual learning. There may be times we feel overwhelmed by the burden of this constant pressure. I find that my connections serve to keep me at the forefront of my industry, as well as help me grow personally and professionally.

I benchmarked with my industry peers to improve continuously as a folding carton manufacturing company. I was part of a business group dedicated to creating a safe place for fellow CEOs to share "issues and challenges" and learn from each other's knowledge and experience. We helped one another grow as people and as corporate presidents. At one point, I became involved with a "Mastermind Group" of fellow women business owners. After attending each meeting, I found I admired those ladies more and more as we drew on each other's wisdom and strength. Collectively and individually, we contributed to each other's growth as women and leaders.

Surrounded by peer connections, I became grounded in the realization of what I do know, rather than focusing on what I do not know. We are not always the best at giving ourselves credit for what we have learned, or how far we have come. Fortunately, our peer connections provide an opportunity to reflect our growth and reaffirm our value.

MAKE DUST

One of my favorite quotes came as a gift to me from a former employee with a note that read, "I saw this, and it reminded me so much of you that I just had to send it." Enclosed was a poster with cowboys on horseback charging to the crest of a hilltop. The caption read, "If you don't make dust, you eat dust."

For years now, this rendition of H. Jackson Brown Jr.'s famous quote has graced the wall of my office in some form or another. It's a constant reminder: If you are going to stay ahead of the pack, Jan, you have got to stay connected.

While I may have had the fortune to inherit a business opportunity with $1.3 in annual sales, the most valuable thing Dad left me is that well-worn piece of advice: "Connect with your industry peers. It's a great way to learn and build trusting relationships. They'll be there for you in case of a disaster." Over 30 years and nearly $38 million in annual sales later, his advice worked.

The connections I had established over the years proved to be extremely helpful as I considered selling the business. The sound wisdom I received from my attorney, CPA, and even my banker, was invaluable. The trusting relationships that had been built by "joining forces" provided the support and sage advice necessary to succeed with the process—and believe me, selling a business is a process.

CONNECTION CHALLENGE

Take note of how often you met with these key connections last fiscal year and evaluate for the coming year.

Industry Peers _____

Position Peers _____

Banker _____

CPA _____

Attorney _____

Customers _____

Family _____

SUGGESTED CONNECTION ACTIONS

Become involved with groups of your peers (industry or position-related or both). Join a group that is already established or start your own. Accountability is a potent part of the growth and learning process.

Determine whether your bank is the perfect partner for your business today and tomorrow. If you are not 100 percent sure, put your banking out for bid. If you are confident, calendar meetings for the rest of your fiscal year.

Take your attorney out to breakfast or lunch so you can get to know each other better. Let them know your goals and objectives. (Yes, you will pay—but off their billing clock!)

Calendar at least two meetings each fiscal year with your CPA—one about halfway through the year and the second at least two months before your year closes. The second one is like the two-minute warning in football, giving you final strategies for the year.

Schedule time with your top customers to engage in a strategic conversation. Find out what their plans are for the future and strategize how you can help them achieve their goals.

Plan a fun event with your family.

NOTES

14

Part *of*
The Journey
Amanda Secola

*"Connections…for a Reason,
for a Season, for a Lifetime"*

Anonymous

Early in my career, I joined a service organization for business and professional women. We agreed to come together to utilize our time, talents, and treasures for the greater good of improving the lives of women and girls. The relationships I formed within this organization have weathered many storms, nurtured my personal growth in a non-threatening environment, and facilitated my learning curve in the areas of leadership. In this group of women, I learned to share without fear of negative repercussions. We built a haven for our team to grow, share, and project the message of women helping women. Maintaining a deep level of intimacy among men or women is never easy. The ultimate component for success is trust.

Ground rules were in place to send the message "what happens here stays here." We accepted the inevitability that we may need to "agree to disagree" yet we work in concert with any decisions reached by consensus. Once having achieved these standards, a foundation for greatness was built. In this chapter, I will present strategies gathered from a combination of education, background, statistical analysis, and data capture, as well as personal and professional experience to assist anyone seeking comfort within the world of connections.

"When Bad Things Happen to Good People"
RABBI HAROLD S. KUSHNER

◂▴▸

INTENTIONS VS. REALITY

I have learned that our best-laid plans can be interrupted by circumstances out of our control and through no fault of our own. Tragedy can change our connection conduit and cause a short in the wiring for a time. I interject the concept of reality as it may blindside us on our journey.

In 2001, I was a senior member of a successful advertising, marketing, and communications agency specializing in the medical device and diagnostic industry. My responsibilities required extensive travel throughout the U.S., meeting existing and potential clients as well as working and attending trade shows and conferences.

At the end of August that year, my only child Blake, age twenty, was in an accident caused by another driver under the influence of narcotics. The world as I knew it stopped. Hospitals, doctors, and family became my focus. Blake lost his life from the injuries he incurred due to the accident. Suddenly, everything I knew to be true and right in the world became suspect. All my friends, family members, personal and professional colleagues, and associates took on a different level of meaning in this newly created world. My journey became a life interrupted. As I share, connect, and reach out to others, I realize each one of us experience tragedy, and it molds the makeup of our connections in the world.

The connections I had previously built were now permanently changed. We never know when tragedy may strike. However, if it does, you may experience a tremendous shift in priorities. Within the eighteen months following Blake's death, many factors led me to change my career path. I made definite distinctions regarding which types of people I was willing to interact with, where I would allow myself to work, and within what channels I would share my skills, talents, and abilities. This newfound philosophy and worldview were born out of a therapeutic analysis of my very existence—my toleration levels, my coping mechanisms, and my survival. The world I had previously known virtually closed in around me. I had to insulate myself against future pain. I went from an extremely outgoing "Type A" personality to an introvert only wanting to interact with a select group of people. That select group became my lifeline.

"When the going gets tough, the tough get going."
JOSEPH P. KENNEDY

◄▲►

Financially, I needed to get back to work and find a position that would allow me to function successfully within my newly-defined individual parameters. I received many lucrative offers, yet I was hesitant to accept any not aligned with my current worldview. After several months, I felt fortunate finally to click with a property management company specializing in senior housing. I was delighted to be able to utilize my skills in corporate marketing for the good of older adults.

Each industry and culture have an unlimited supply of connections, subcultures, and dynamics that provide the foundation and engine for groups to find common objectives. I had successfully cracked into the senior housing market through referrals. Once hired, I worked directly under the vice president. Her willingness to delegate and share essential duties provided ample educational opportunities for me to learn this vertical market.

I attribute much of my success to the level of confidence she carried, her collaborative management style, and the non-competitive nature of our relationship. I immersed myself working as a marketing analyst for this dynamic group of business professionals. My position offered a tremendous prospect for professional growth within a compelling and vital industry. I embraced both the executive connections and an empowering and promising environment for the future.

Several years later, I founded Senior Industry Professionals, Incorporated. It began successfully with several clients secured from those valuable connections. As a female entrepreneur, my business is now totally reliant on my ability to make winning connections at various levels. Building on valued connections is the genius behind ongoing success today and what I contend is the "application" of knowledge.

THE 'APPLICATION' OF KNOWLEDGE IS POWER

An educator once said, "Knowledge is Power." Many of us embraced this philosophy throughout our lives and became life-long learners. Yet, at one point, a professional revelation hits us with, "It's not *what* you know, it's *who* you know." Although not a new philosophy, utilizing connections as currency is becoming a mainstream marketing tool. Connecting is a compelling concept that merges our competencies with our ability to communicate. When we become willing to share our lives, talents, and stories with others, we are wisely *applying* what we know, and this becomes the *power* behind our successes and our failures.

Scientific methodology has at its core a process of trial and error. Connections are similar in scope. Let's take a scientific look at a chamber of commerce mixer...where a variety of business owners and professionals mix and mingle. Marketing professionals will set a goal or ask themselves before the mixer, "What is my expected outcome from this interaction?" The answer simply put would be, "Make a connection with at least one company we can do business with in the future."

The product or service your company offers begins an elimination process. For instance, your offering is likely to benefit perhaps 50 percent of the mixer's attendees in their personal or professional worlds. You will first need to meet all attendees to make an initial connection and determine which business concerns they represent, of which only a small percentage may immediately be in the market for your offering. Out of that group, you may be able to obtain one future meeting. If this is your result, congratulations are in order! Remember, the initial objective was to make one connection with future business possibilities.

However, we cannot stop there. Each of those connections could lead to yet another. A positive step has been taken to help promote you and your business. Even though you are not currently in those connections' immediate inner circles, your initial meeting has left a good impression. When that individual runs into an associate who expresses an interest or need for the types of goods or services you offer, she realizes sharing your information is in her best interest. You may ask, "Why would I share if I do not have a personal testimony?" An important observation is to note that you will want others to do the same for you.

Just because you share a contact does not mean you are giving an endorsement. Leaving that unsaid is okay. You are only providing an opportunity for interaction. Not only that, your stature has changed within the dynamic of your colleague relationship. Now you are viewed as a connector and a resource for this associate.

"Business networking is the art of
turning contacts into contracts."

RHONDA SHER

◄▲►

UNDERSTANDING THE GROUP DYNAMIC

Making connections or networking through business mixers and groups has become standard procedure across most industries. A tremendous number of networking groups exist today that use business classifications as a defining tool. This means only one business per classification is allowed into a group in a specific region. An example would be a printing company. Once that class of business has paid its dues, then no other printer can join. Annual dues are expected, and quite often, additional monthly dues are required. The concept is that each company will support, work with, promote, and utilize the goods or services of the other business types in the group. Experience has revealed that the price point of your service or product offering will be a determining factor in return on investment.

If you are not familiar with the "pay-to-play" networking or connection by classification groups, here's how it works. If you are an exterminating service provider, the first year in a group you may find your company providing services for almost every member. This group may be an excellent resource for your company for at least two years. However, unless the group continues to grow and bring in new members, over time your ability to attract new clients through this group will most likely be diminished. However, networking groups can deploy enhancements that may allow for continued growth...ambassadors, city involvement, and community event participation, etc. These types of activities can extend the life of your ability to derive business from this group dynamic.

Occasionally, a few annoyances may be present in this type of organized body. Obstacles to growth may be curtailed by one of the members having a less than positive experience and then spreading negative comments about you or your company. The group can avoid this by setting ground rules ranging from business protocol to sharing information about personal interactions. Keeping the mission statement in the forefront helps everyone stay focused on accomplishing the goals of the group.

> *"Connections today can be used as social currency."*
>
> JUDY GOFFIN

◂▴▸

The chamber of commerce from our earlier example provides another opportunity. Its function is to offer businesses a chance to have a place to come together and share information about their goods and services. However, this is an old model that I have found inconsistent with today's business world. The effectiveness of the chamber has much bearing on the city it represents. Experience shows that well-run cities do not necessarily indicate well-run chambers.

Additionally, support for a chamber and its budget is different in every area, so I recommend visiting each chamber in the areas you want to do business. Analyze its effectiveness by first interviewing the executive director, attending a few meetings, and talking with other involved members. Local business owners are savvy about what helps them; they will let you know by their attendance or absence whether they believe the group is helping them grow.

Trade associations and service organizations provide additional ways to spread the word about your goods and services. Typically, trade associations shout the loudest for more substantial contributors, which means if your company joins at the highest dues level, it will receive a more significant amount of the promotional pie, if you will.

AS THE JOURNEY CONTINUES...

It is important to note that our ability to connect changes as we age or as we advance in our careers. My specific area of expertise is working with and developing strategies to connect within the fifty-plus age group. Our lifestyles have the propensity to change after age fifty, and that can impact our relationships and connections. Our inner circles may become smaller, yet our need for connection continues and often becomes greater. Many factors impact this time in life. Family dynamics, professional accomplishments, retirement concerns, career path options, college-bound children, and aging parents can all impact our present reality and our long-term goals.

When considering the science of making connections, focus on outcomes and return on investment, but never discount the importance of peace of mind, reliability, loyalty, and honesty. Women tend to more easily develop enriching relationships, whether personal or professional, than men. However, making connections is an integral part of life for us all, no matter our age or gender.

This second half of life also brings an opportunity to assess where we have been, where we are, and where we want to go before hitting that "finish line!" Many find this phase of life extremely enlightening and recognize the connections we have made up to this point become paramount to our future adventures and endeavors. Unity and connection are interwoven throughout the universe in all things.

The movie, *Six Degrees of Separation*, showed we are never far from making potentially life-changing connections. Those of us using social networks are aware of the numbers associated with how many "friends or associates" we currently have and the potential number we could have based on those connections. The opportunity to connect is within our grasp. The depth of our connections is what makes us thrive. The people we touch come into our lives and cross our paths sometimes for a reason, sometimes for a season, and sometimes for a lifetime.

Whatever your desires are for the future, know they can be realized or enhanced through connections. Whether you are just starting out at twenty or you are starting again at sixty, successful plans always include the need to connect with someone else. Friends, relatives, co-workers, associates, partners, and acquaintances will all become part of your success and your failure. Ask yourself, "Do I want to start my own business? Work full-time? Volunteer? Go back to school?" I guarantee once you answer the question, the next thing you do will be making a connection.

"Receive joy every day with an attitude of gratitude."

M. J. RYAN

◄▲►

DO UNTO OTHERS AS YOU WOULD HAVE THEM DO UNTO YOU

One caution: The connection process should not be confused with using or manipulating people in a conniving, negative way. Connecting is all about positive, compassionate attitudes that foster collaborative, intelligent projects for valuable outcomes in the world. This form of business building can be extremely rewarding. Use your energy and personality in conversation to express excitement about possibilities for future contracts and collaborations. Welcome human interaction through existing connections; utilize technology by performing research through the Internet; and make contacts through local, city, county, and state organizations.

The resources available continually change in our environment today. Computers, cell phones, and digital reading devices are part of the landscape helping us stay connected. Keep in mind a successful connection is one that ultimately leads you to a form of revenue or connection currency.

CONNECTION CHALLENGE

Here is your opportunity to broaden your circle of influence. Identify three new groups that might provide you with a chance to grow personally or professionally. The groups you select should:

- Provide exposure to potentially ten new contacts or connections

- Create valuable resources for your inevitable success

- Show promise for a potentially new revenue stream

With these things in mind, check your calendar and see where you can work something new into your schedule. Think of it as a custom-designed self-improvement class!

NOTES

_____

_____

_____

_____

_____

_____

_____

_____

_____

_____

_____

_____

_____

_____

_____

_____

_____

_____

_____

_____

_____

_____

_____

_____

_____

_____

_____

_____

Conclusion

Creating *a* Legacy *of* Connection

"We have dreamed it: therefore it is. I have become convinced that everything we think and feel is merely perception: that our lives–individually as well as communally–are molded around such perception: and that if we want to change, we must alter our perception. When we give our energy to a different dream, the world is transformed. To create a new world, we must first create a new dream."

JOHN PERKINS

Cultural myths often demand we do whatever it takes to get ahead. We have to be willing to let go of any lie as it limits our possibilities. We can choose to act differently and make use of circumstances – good or bad. When people choose connections based on their deepest, most soulful interests and commitments, those connections can become lasting and can catalyze their lives and the lives of those around them.

In the 1970's, the American engineer, author, and futurist R. Buckminster ("Bucky") Fuller spoke about the myths in basic science that blocked us from an accurate vision of the world. He spoke about evolution from a "you-or-me world"—a world where either you or I make it and where we need to compete and fight to see who wins—to a "you-and-me world" where all of us succeed. I continue to believe in a world where connecting enables us to share our wealth, community and prosperity.

"The journey of 1000 miles starts with a single step."

LAO-TZU

◄▲►

Imagine a world where we all focus on making a difference by sharing gifts, abilities, talents, and experiences. Partnering with others to expand and deepen our lives would certainly bridge the gaps that often divide us—race, gender, skin tone, physicality, age, religion, socioeconomic status, and sexual preference.

DESIGNING MY DESTINY

Our lives are always either growing and expanding or stuck and shrinking. Do we live our lives doing what we have always done, expecting different results? Or, do we actively seek new paths for living out our unique purpose?

"Were there none who were discontented with what they have, the world would never reach for anything better."

FLORENCE NIGHTINGALE

◄▲►

Fast-forwarding through the process, I envision the service of connecting as a benefit to organizations that are doing incredible good in the world. Because of my background in leadership development, I understand the importance of having a thought-out plan. I have also discovered that while the plan is critical to know where you are going, getting quiet and listening are not passive activities but rather bold undertakings that can sprout wings. The power that comes from being an authentic connector can do the same for your world. Are you up for the challenge?

THE FINAL CONNECTION CHALLENGE

Make connection a priority in your life. Actively set aside time to connect with one person every day. If you consistently execute this action, you will open the door to new potential partnerships and deepen existing connections, yielding phenomenal results.

NOTES

About the Authors

"Strong women—precious jewels all—their humanness is evident in their accessibility. We are able to enter into the spirit of these women and rejoice in their warmth and courage."

Maya Angelou

JANET CERVANTES-HAGEMAN

Janet Cervantes-Hageman is the Chief Financial Officer of Eck Automotive Group based in Wichita, Kansas. She has been in the retail automotive industry for thirty years. Janet is a leader in her community and her church and she volunteers for numerous charity organizations.

She currently is the President of the Midwest Chapter of the Leukemia & Lymphoma Society in Wichita, Kansas, the Executive Director of the Adopt A School Organization and President of the Mike Cervantes Stroke Awareness Foundation. She started the F.A.S.T. 5K run on behalf of her husband's foundation that has become part of the American Heart & Stroke Association's Heart Walk. She has helped raise millions of dollars for various groups. She has an active leadership role in St. Elizabeth Ann Seton Catholic Church and has served on decision-making committees with the Maize School District and City of Wichita's benchmarking committee.

Janet and her husband Gary enjoy spending time with their family, which includes three children, two daughters-in-law, and three grandchildren. They like traveling and are both sports enthusiasts.

◂▴▸

LYNN FORESE

Lynn Forese is a Senior Practice Leader driving business development and client service for a global professional services firm with an emphasis in business transformation initiatives. Lynn has a BS in accounting and an MBA. She has successfully led business transformation efforts by integrating people, processes, and systems.

Lynn, a single mother, residing in Los Angeles, California, draws on more than twenty-five years of broad experience in information technology, change management, and business process re-engineering.

◄▲►

TINA LEE

Tina Lee is Co-owner of Chew Lee Accounting Group and Chew & Lee Financial. She has more than 20 years of experience in a wide range of accounting, tax and financial services.

Tina is passionate about life and living it to the fullest. She believes the right kind of connecting & networking makes business and friend connections, as well as love and spiritual connections.

Tina takes joy in being a leader in her field. She is a Past President of the National Association of Women Business Owners, Wichita Chapter, has served as the Kansas State Director for the National Society of Accountants and is a Past President of The Public Accountants Association of Kansas.

Tina has been involved in the grassroots development of several women-business organizations, serves on the Operations Council of her Church and participated in Habitat for Humanity Women Build.

◄▲►

DIXIE MCDANIEL DE ANDRADE

Dixie McDaniel de Andrade is founder and President of "Envision Possibilities" an Andrade Ventures Inc. company, focusing on life purpose coaching and strength training personal consulting. Her passion for and commitment to helping women live purposefully using their natural strengths and values is evident in her coaching and her life.

Active in her spiritual community, Dixie strives to live each day authentically and abundantly. She is also a representative for Compass Inc., a personal development and coaching network. Her passion is to inspire, empower, and connect women. She previously worked more than ten years in international development and training for non-governmental organizations and non-profits in Washington, D.C and overseas.

Dixie is happily married; she and her husband reside in Jacksonville, Florida, with their identical twin boys.

◄▲►

CARRIE C. O'CONNOR

Carrie C. O'Connor, ARM-P, CSRM grew up in Northern California as the daughter of a teacher and businessman. She is a Partner in the law firm of O'Connor * Telezinski, Attorneys at Law, a law firm whose emphasis is representation for workers' compensation defense—primarily for large governmental entities, including school districts, cities, and counties.

The California State Bar certifies Carrie as a Legal Specialist in Workers' Compensation Law. She is also a Certified School Risk Manager. Carrie and her partner provide various legal services to small businesses in their local business community. She strives to keep her clients abreast of the newest changes in the law and is an advocate for preventing fraud in workers' compensation. Carrie is also the author of many industry articles for claims professionals. She currently lives in Norco, California with her husband and son. Her hobbies include ballroom dancing and social networking.

◂▴▸

LINDA REIFSCHNEIDER

Linda Reifschneider has thirty years of experience in marketing and teaching. Retired now, and living in southern Colorado, Linda stays busy in her cherished small-town community. She shares her talents by working part-time for the local telephone company and generously serving as a substitute librarian.

Linda's main focus is the ministry she and her husband of over twenty-five years, began in 2010. Lion Chasers, a 501-C3 nonprofit, was formed with the goal of leading short-term mission trips internationally to improve the lives of others. At this printing, the pair have traveled with nearly fifteen teams to Central America where they have built churches, which double as schools, in some of the poorest regions of that continent.

Being careful not to reproduce the "too busy" lifestyle of her pre-retirement years, Linda remains active in her community with select volunteer projects. She supports charitable organizations such as Greenhorn Valley Baptist Church, Compassion International, International Ministries, Global Doves, and Spirit West Coast.

◂▴▸

AMANDA BLAKE SECOLA

Amanda Blake Secola is Editor/Publisher of *Not Born Yesterday!*, the Voice of Southern California Seniors and CEO/President, Senior Industry Professionals, Inc.

Her career has included comprehensive marketing, sales, and public relations work within diverse industries. In each vertical or niche market, client profiling would include cultural norms, behavior projections, response analytics, and outcomes.

For more than twenty years, Amanda has given concentrated effort to working within the senior living and the healthcare arena. She established Senior Industry Professionals, Inc. in 2008, and in 2009, she became publisher for the fifty-plus publication, *Not Born Yesterday!* Her firm works with clients establishing business-to-business and/or business-to-consumer level programs, depending on their needs and objectives.

◄▲►

JANET STEINER

Janet Steiner has been President and CEO of Thoro Packaging since her father stepped down in 1982. She is held in high regard as a leader of an innovative and successful folding carton company. Jan's passion is creating beautiful folding carton packaging for Thoro's customers.

Jan is known and often recognized for her enthusiasm, creativity, and "Can Do" attitude. She is a sought-after speaker and panelist and is a frequent presenter at many business and community events. Jan has been recognized for many of her contributions by local and national organizations, including receiving the Business Woman of the Year award from the National Association of Women Business Owners-IE.

Ralph Waldo Emerson said, "Do not go where the path may lead, go instead where there is no path and leave a trail." Janet Steiner rarely takes the path. As a woman president in a predominantly male industry, she has spent the past thirty years blazing many a trail.

◂▲▸

LYNDA-ROSS VEGA

Lynda-Ross has a passion for helping people discover and apply their natural talents in everything they do. With Gary M. Jordan, Ph. D., she co-developed Perceptual Style® Theory, a revolutionary phycological assessment and personal development system that helps people unleash their potential and master effective communications with the people in their lives.

Her road to success began in corporate America in the mid-'70s where she first developed her interest in helping people maximize their effectiveness and their enjoyment in what they do. A lifelong student of human behavior, her research and application of style theories in business led to her collaboration with Dr. Jordan beginning in 1983.

Lynda-Ross and her husband, Ricardo, launched their own consulting company in 1996 which continues to thrive.

◂▴▸

BECKY WHATLEY

Becky Whatley "grew up" in the printing industry, spending more than 25 years working for her family's printing company before branching out to public relations and communications. Currently working for the Inland Empire's leading PR firm, Becky specializes in advocacy and community outreach for land use and re-development projects.

Becky consults with small businesses, nonprofits, and political campaigns to design and implement successful marketing strategies with effective promotional materials. Her clarity in message, eye for design, and ability to cut through clutter helps her transform what clients bring into award-winning materials that exceed their expectations.

Leading with her heart, Becky enjoys championing young women, as a Big Sister in Big Brothers Big Sisters, Inland Empire Chapter and mentor to high school juniors in the Education Academy at her alma mater, John W. North High School in Riverside, California.

◄▲►

CYNTHIA WRIGHT

Cynthia Wright is currently the Executive Director of the Fox Riverside Theater Foundation in Riverside, California. She served as an independent contractor for non-profits through her business, The Wright Image, and previously served as Associate Vice President for Institutional Advancement at California Baptist University.

Her volunteer work includes serving the City of Riverside's Human Relations Commission, the Mayor's Multicultural Forum, the Greater Riverside Chambers of Commerce (Leadership Riverside, Magnolia Area Business Council, Downtown Business Council), the American Heart Association's Go Red for Women Executive Leadership Team, and she previously served on the Board of the Orange County/Inland Empire Chapter of the Leukemia & Lymphoma Society (LLS). In 2011-12, she participated in the Environmental Leadership Academy, a collaboration of Cal State San Marcos and the Community Foundation, serving Riverside and San Bernardino Counties.

◄▲►

KATHERINE A. WRIGHT, ED. D.

Katherine A. Wright (Kathy) spent 37 years as a teacher and administrator in public education. In her last year of service, she held the position of superintendent and proudly led a Southern California school district of 20,000 students who are largely English Learners and from disadvantaged backgrounds to higher levels of achievement.

In retirement, Kathy is involved in numerous nonprofit and civic activities including arts organizations, higher education, historical societies and philanthropic endeavors serving children and teens. She has received many awards and recognitions including Athena of Riverside, Alumnus of the Year at Riverside Community College District, Distinguished Alumnus of the Year at University of California Riverside, Outstanding Alumna at the University of California Riverside Graduate School of Education, Riverside Downtown Partnership Volunteer of the Year award and the Scholarship America National Volunteer of the Year award.

◄▲►

About the Anthologist

LISA MARIE PLATSKE

Lisa Marie Platske left her action-packed life as a Federal law enforcement officer to become the CEO of international leadership training and consulting company, **Upside Thinking, Inc.**

An award-winning leadership expert, Lisa Marie uses her law enforcement journey which began on the piers in New York and ended post 9/11 to deliver presentations centered on her seven-step leadership process focused on connection, positioning, and executive presence. She shares what exceptional leaders do differently, why connection is the new currency, and how to build a winning strategy to get big opportunities.

A certified master coach, Lisa Marie has coached mission-driven managers and executives from three continents and in over thirty industries including healthcare, real estate, technology, financial planning, law, and insurance on how to position their expertise using her 7 Pillars of Leadership™. Her proven success strategies have resulted in her clients being leaders worth following as they create positive changes in behavior within their organization. Simply put, Lisa Marie creates effective leaders.

She has delivered leadership training and coached managers and executives for clients from corporate and government entities such as Honeywell, State Farm Insurance, BAXA Healthcare, the Department of Homeland Security, the Federal Energy Regulatory Commission, Pacific Gas & Electric, the Ontario Convention Center, and Perry Ellis International.

Lisa Marie earned a BS in Criminal Justice and an MA in Human Resources Training and Development with a thesis on the benefits of formal vs. informal mentoring. She has a certification in leadership, has been featured in numerous television, radio and print media outlets. She is the author of six books including the #1 international best seller, *Turn Possibilities into Realities.*

In 2016, Lisa Marie was recognized by the International Alliance of Women as one of the top 100 Women Making a Difference in the world. She is a member of the Forbes Coaches Council and serves on the executive board of Project Forgive as well as the executive advisory council for Leadership California. The founder of Design Your Destiny Live (www.DesignYourDestinyLive.com), Lisa Marie lives in Alexandria, VA with her loving and supportive husband, Jim, and their two pet foxes. Connected to God, Lisa Marie listens and lets Him lead.

◄▲►

www.ingramcontent.com/pod-product-compliance
Lightning Source LLC
Chambersburg PA
CBHW060552210326
41519CB00014B/3449